SEEKING ARRANGEMENT:

THE DEFINITIVE GUIDE TO SUGAR DADDY AND MUTUALLY BENEFICIAL RELATIONSHIPS

Brandon Wade

IVY STREET PRESS

What people are saying...

This is a book that gives the reader more options than a traditional relationship and teaches the reader how to negotiate what they really want out of the mutually beneficial relationship - up front- so that both parties know what is expected going into it.

—Donna Spangler, author of
How to Get a Rich Man:
The Princess Formula

Let's not forget the simplicity of what Brandon Wade offers men and women: relationships based on mutual respect and trust. If all relationships were like this, there would be a lot less heart break and a lot more happy people in the world!

—Alan Bentley, author of
Crack the Guy Code

As the Queen of Spotting the Kooks, I found Brandon's expose of the "neo sugar daddy" a provocative twist on how relationships are evolving with the times. This book pulls no punches, and leaves it up to the reader to decide whether making "arrangements" is kooky, kinky, or cool.

—Adryenn Ashley, Award Winning Author of
Every Single Girl's Guide to Her Future
Husband's Last Divorce and *Spotting the Kooks*

Seeking Arrangement opened my eyes to a kind of relationship I would have thought incompatible with female independence, when it's actually the opposite. This lucid guide shatters old stereotypes, letting the reader come to her own conclusions, not just about Sugar Daddies and Sugar Babies, but about all kinds of relationships. I wish I'd had this information twenty years ago, when I really could have made use of it!

—Marcy Sheiner, writer and editor of
Herotica and Best Women's Erotica

"For girls looking to maximize on the men who will adore them, this book is for you!"

—Leidra Lawson, author of
Sugar Daddy 101

Kudos to Brandon Wade for delving into this rarely discussed, under-the-sheets lifestyle and making sense of it all – eliminating many of the misconceptions, intimidation and fear associated with this subject. The book is a FAQs gold mine for the adventurous, a primer for the cautious, and a riveting read for the curious.

—Linda Bona, freelance writer and
former Editor of
Tuned In Magazine (San Diego)

Anyone wanting to break free of old relationship paradigms should read this lucid guide to Sugar Daddy/Sugar Baby arrangements. The author paints a vivid picture of a world most people don't even know exists. With new, almost revolutionary, ideas about love, sex and romance, this guide offers fresh solutions to the age-old puzzle of romantic relationships.

—Alicia Dunams, author of
*Goal Digger: Lessons Learned
from the Rich Men I Dated*

'Seeking Arrangement' pulls no punches: not every relationship is about hearts and flowers, and if some people are willing to pay for sex and companionship, while others are willing to offer it, why not? This book is a welcome concept for anybody who's ever been too shy to confess they crave a Daddy, Mama, or Baby. Talk about liberating!

—Sage Vivant, author of
Your Erotic Personality
and founder of CustomEroticaSource.com
www.sagevivant.com

Mr. Wade has clearly explained this alternative lifestyle of being a Sugar Daddy or Baby. It allows for both parties to negotiate their desires. Try it, you might like it.

—Ilona Paris, author of
Hot Cougar Sex and *You Know You Love It:
Lessons in Sexual Mischief*

Copyright (©) 2009 InfoStream Group, Inc.

Published by:
Ivy Street Press
6781 South Eastern Avenue Suite A
Las Vegas, NV 89119

ISBN-13: 978-0-9910089-2-6

Library of Congress Control Number: 2009921768

Printed in the United States of America

Seeking Arrangement May 2009

10 9 8 7 6 5 4 3 2

I dedicate this book to my wife Yuliya
who showed me how to love and to live.

Table of Contents

Introduction

Since the coming of the Internet, people who share common interests or characteristics can exchange information with the click of a mouse. Soon a whole new generation won't know there was once a time when finding like-minded people wasn't this easy, especially if you differed in any way from social norms. Your difference could be completely benign – like having nine toes instead of ten – but if you didn't know anyone else with nine toes, you felt like a freak. You felt isolated and alone.

The generation now coming of age won't even be able to imagine that terrible sense of isolation. Now, every kind of life or lifestyle variation, every permutation, every possible minority—gays, dwarf lovers, people with freckles—you name it, there's an online group, or more likely a dozen. People who share the same characteristic, condition, interest or desire can write to and read about and learn from each other. Nobody, no matter how small or great their interest or deviation from the mainstream, need live in isolation ever again.

In 2006 I launched SeekingArrangement.com, a website for people interested in "sugar" relationships—that is, relationships based on an exchange of assets. By "exchange of assets" I'm referring to money on one side, and various types of companionship on the other. Commonly referred to as Sugar Daddy/Sugar Baby relationships, these are usually formed between an older man and a younger woman—but the reverse (Mama/Baby) also exists.

I saw a need for this service because I knew people who quietly lived the Sugar lifestyle. I suspected there were a lot more out there who fantasized or thought seriously about forming such attachments, but had no idea how to begin or where to find partners.

Because our society tends to frown upon alternative relationship arrangements, those who live the Sugar lifestyle are often stigmatized and made to feel ashamed. Curious Sugar wanna-bes are frequently embarrassed by their secret desires. Without a presence on the Internet (or anywhere else), these people felt isolated.

A few years back, an extremely successful older gentleman I know and I were admiring the charms of a gorgeous young woman. Whimsically I said, "I wonder what it takes to get something like that?" He looked at me and said, "Oh, about five to ten gee's a month." And then he told me about the four Sugar Babies he's had over the course of his lifetime.

My interest in creating SeekingArrangement.com emerged organically from my life experience. Throughout my school years, including college, I was considered an intellectual. I was the quintessential nerd who participated in all the science fairs and Mathematics Olympiads, but I was heartbreakingly shy around members of the opposite sex. I didn't have a girlfriend until I was nineteen and a sophomore at MIT. Like many of my peers, I idolized Hugh Hefner and looked to him as a model – successful, handsome, and, most importantly, he's always had beautiful women at his side: Hef is never without one or more gorgeous girlfriends.

After graduating and completing my MBA I became a management consultant, then later on a senior executive at a Fortune 10 company, and finally an entrepreneur. Over the years I've joined numerous dating websites, only to be disappointed by the results. With a higher ratio of males to females, and a disproportionate number of testosterone-filled men competing for the attention of a comparatively few beautiful women, my messages were seldom returned.

It was out of frustration with conventional dating websites that the idea for SeekingArrangement.com was born. Here, intelligence, success and wealth count as much, or more than, superficial qualities such as physical appearance, well-toned pecs, or being up on the latest trendy trends. Here, guys who've worked hard, achieved success, and want to savor the fruits of their labor have as much of a shot, or better, at attracting high-quality women. The ratio of women to men is much greater on SeekingArrangement than on other websites, and in a smaller pool, I'm a bigger fish: guys like me stand out as gentlemen. The women on the site value our assets, and shower us with attention. SeekingArrangement is my attempt to level the playing field.

Although I'd always had a vague idea that others like myself existed – that there were people quietly living a Sugar lifestyle and others who wanted to – I thought their number was fairly small. My goal was simply to put potential Sugar Daddies and Babies in touch, and to ease their isolation. I had absolutely no idea how many Daddies would want to connect online. I didn't know if they'd welcome SeekingArrangement, or see it as an invasion of privacy.

I had a pretty good idea, though, that a good number of Sugar Baby wanna-bes would show up. All my life I've heard women speak longingly about wanting to be cared for, financially and otherwise. In a world where women earn seventy-seven cents to every dollar earned by a man, I've seen countless women struggle to put themselves through school, set up professional careers, raise children alone or just survive from one day to the next. Like everyone else, I was familiar with their laundry list of complaints against men – slackers who lack ambition, guys who sit around Starbucks with their laptops, writing a screenplay for the next *Titanic,* or banging out The Great American Novel for seven or eight years, with no end in sight.

Throughout history, older men of wealth have traditionally taken on the responsibility of caring for younger women. Whether confirmed bachelors or married with mistresses, men of a certain age and financial standing have always mentored, supported and helped young women in exchange for favors, sexual and otherwise. Until the existence of the Internet, though, these couplings were random, risky, and often rife with misunderstanding and drama. Now, with a platform where Sugar Babies and Daddies can meet, express their needs up front, and come to equable terms, these arrangements need not be random or *too* risky (let's face it, there's some risk in every relationship, no matter how well-planned).

Right around the time I was hatching my website plan, an intriguing post from Craigslist began circulating on the Internet. It read, in part:

> I'm tired of beating around the bush. I'm a spectacularly beautiful 25 year old girl. I'm articulate and classy...I'm looking to get married to a guy who makes at least half a million a year ...Here are my questions specifically: Where do you single rich men hang out? Give me specifics: bars, restaurants, gyms. What are you looking for in a mate? Be honest guys, you won't hurt my feelings. Is there an age range I should be targeting (I'm 25)? ...Where do the hedge fund guys hang out?

That did it: with everyone talking about this bold "Sugar Baby," and other women confessing they identified with her, I knew the time was ripe for SeekingArrangement.com.

Still, I was not prepared for the response.

Within a year we had over 100,000 members. We've been covered by media all over the U.S. as well as overseas. Some reporters are judgmental, but most treat us as an amusement. One radio host dubbed SeekingArrangement.com "the dating site from Planet Capitalism." CNN called upon a psychological "expert" to weigh in with her opinion: predictably, she said that anyone who'd get into this kind of arrangement has "low self-esteem."

Right. I wonder if that shrink ever met or spoke to a *real* Sugar Baby. I wonder if she's ever seen a drop-dead gorgeous twenty-something gal who carries herself with grace and composure among groups of rich, accomplished men and women, some of whom are a lot older than she is. A woman with low self-esteem would have a difficult time, to say the least, pulling off the Sugar Baby role. It takes self-knowledge and self-respect to hold one's own among social circles of sophisticated, worldly people.

Meanwhile, we've managed to keep a lot of Sugar Daddies, Mamas and Babies very happy. Said one satisfied Baby:

> It's not easy to be a struggling artist in New York City. I am beautiful and single, so I decided to join SeekingArrangement.com to find a Sugar Daddy who could give me a better lifestyle. Less than two weeks after joining the website, I met two eligible benefactors. This dating website really works.

This book is an outgrowth of and companion to the website. It is a guide to Sugar relationships: how to find what you're looking for and attract what you want; how to negotiate a mutually beneficial relationship; how to protect yourself from fakes and scams; how to navigate the world of arranged relationships; and how to make this lifestyle work for you. It is based on information gleaned from hundreds of posts in our discussion forums, and on my own communications and observations with participants from around the world – the people who live the Sugar lifestyle. From Malibu to Orlando, Atlanta to Tokyo, London to Sydney, Australia, we conducted e-mail interviews to learn what motivates people to form Sugar relationships and live the Sugar lifestyle.

In a broader sense, this book is about learning to live the way *you* want to live, rather than the way your parents, teachers, church, or society say you *should*. This book is *not* about Main Street U.S.A. It's about wealthy, beautiful, talented, smart, successful, confident, and powerful people who live life to the max.

Facts: Approximately one in five adults in allegedly monogamous relationships – or 22 percent – have at some point cheated on their partners. According to a survey conducted in April 2007 by MSNBC.com/iVillage, nearly 50% of married people admit to being unfaithful at some point in their lives. Nearly half of all marriages end in divorce.

Despite these statistics, a majority of Americans persist in believing that monogamous marriage is the ideal relationship configuration *for everyone*. I'm not saying monogamy is a bad thing, or that exclusive marriages don't work, or that nobody can possibly be happy in them. I am pointing out that, despite all evidence to the contrary, as a society we exalt monogamy while harshly judging anyone who experiments with other kinds of relationships and lifestyles.

That's what a Sugar arrangement is: another kind of relationship, another kind of lifestyle. It may not be for everyone—but for some people it's a satisfying, ethical way to live. Here are some examples taken directly from member profiles on SeekingArrangement.com:

> Seeking Sugar Daddy to be my mentor, help with small business model and maybe invest in my new venture. We can keep each other company while working on something exciting and profitable for us both.
>
> • • • • •
>
> I am an experienced Sugar Daddy who understands that you have needs beyond a day at the spa and an occasional shopping trip. I am intense in my professional life and easy-going in my personal life. I am athletic, adventurous, successful and generous. I have diverse interests, but particularly enjoy sports, wine collecting, tropical resorts and mountain lodges.
>
> • • • • •
>
> I am looking for someone who is established, stable and generous. Someone with a sense of humor and intellect. Someone who is into the whole give and take type of relationship. Most important, someone who will appreciate my outer and inner beauty.
>
> • • • • •
>
> I'm looking for a woman who is fun-loving, sexual, adventurous and can travel (at least on occasion); a woman who enjoys being pampered, but can also have a good time just drinking margaritas at the beach. I don't live my life on a budget, and I enjoy taking care of someone who makes me happy. I'm not looking for one-time "play dates."
>
> • • • • •
>
> Sugar Baby (Male) and/or Sugar Baby (Female). Although I'm not certain what I'm looking for in this, I do know that I am seeking a quality person to spend time with. I like partying at clubs, but also love a quiet night watching a movie and relaxing. Would like to meet someone who is attractive and smart. I enjoy theatre, concerts, sports, flying, scuba diving, travel. I just don't have anyone to do them with. Interested?

In the ideal Sugar arrangement, both parties get exactly what they want – but this can only come about if they're clear about what that is, as the above ads illustrate. This takes a good degree of self-knowledge; as Joe Jackson sang, *"You can't get what you want till you know what you want."*

It also takes a willingness to tell the other person what that is, honestly and up front. Ironically, one of the reasons men and women embrace the Sugar lifestyle is that, in order to practice it, you have to negotiate, and in order to negotiate, you have to tell the truth. To quote another lyricist, *"To live outside the law you must be honest."* (Bob Dylan)

Strangers to alternative lifestyles are sometimes shocked by the bold, up-front language used in Sugar ads. To their inexperienced ears it sounds vaguely kinky, so they assume these people behave in unethical or underhanded ways. Nothing could be further from the truth. Browsing through a site like SeekingArrangement.com reveals a high degree of ethics among participants, who repeat like a mantra, *No Strings, No Games.*

Thus, if you thought this book might show you how to use or manipulate the opposite sex, you might as well stop reading right now. There's a world of difference between negotiation and manipulation. When we talk about Sugar Babies, we're not referring to the old stereotype of the gold-digger who takes a man for everything she can get out of him in exchange for sex. Nor are we talking about male gigolos who prey on wealthy older women, or lecherous elderly Sugar Daddies stalking young innocent victims. Erase those hackneyed images from your mind right now.

We're talking about strong, successful men and women who know what they want and set out to get it. Their happiness doesn't come *at the expense of* someone else, but rather *in sync with* another person. When one person's needs dovetail with another's, everyone gets what they want and nobody gets hurt.

Thanks to the Internet and a number of societal changes, the Sugar lifestyle appears to be gaining in popularity. Some say it's a backlash to feminism – that men and women are tired of resisting what they call *Mother Nature* - and using Sugar arrangements as an excuse to revert to antiquated gender roles. Others say it's a logical outgrowth of feminism – that when women achieve more independence and freedom, they can choose the kinds of relationships they want without fear of dire consequences.

At SeekingArrangement.com we say it's a logical lifestyle for independent-minded 21st century individuals. Instead of following outdated scripts written by your ancestors, you can choose to create a life that suits you and you alone. For those who want to experiment with alternative relationships, this book will serve as a guide. The Sugar lifestyle is for people who, rather than drifting into a marriage of necessity or convenience, actively negotiate for what they want out of life. This book will show you how to dip into the Sugar Bowl – and stay there.

As for those who wouldn't go near the Sugar Bowl with a ten-foot teaspoon, but are curious and open-minded, I hope this book will give you a newfound respect for the Sugar lifestyle and the people who practice it.

Note: It is not unheard of for an older wealthy woman to want the same kind of relationship as her male counterparts, whether with a male or female Sugar Baby, but because their numbers are small, I rarely refer to them specifically. Unless otherwise stated, however, Sugar Mamas are implicitly included in the umbrella term *Sugar Daddies*. Similarly, male Sugar Babies are included under the *Sugar Baby* umbrella, even though *Babies* or *Babes* are almost exclusively referred to here as female; and finally, gay relationships, also part of the Sugar community, fall into the respective categories of Sugar Daddy/Sugar Baby.

CHAPTER ONE:

THEY LIVE AMONG US

I'm a very busy man – no time for games. I need a female that can carry herself well in public. Her looks must cause men to stop and stare when she's on my arm. In return she'll be pampered, share what I have to offer, and go out for fun times. All our meetings will be on the road except for the first. We will never meet in Chicago.

· · · · ·

Young enough for fun and adventure, old enough to have made my fortune already in the dot-com universe. I'm looking for a fun and sexy girl to spoil. I am not looking for a serious relationship but I also don't want a girl who has several sugar daddies – just one, and that's me. Intelligent, fun-loving, and sensual a must.

> I am a good-looking, healthy 50-year-old. I have worked hard all my life, and as a result have acquired all the trappings – big house, boats, a plane, etc. I have also been knocked around enough to know all these things are of no value without the right person to share them. I'm looking for a young, fun, caring, beautiful blond blue-eyed girl. I am open to any kind of arrangement. If we meet, I will be charming and you will have a great time.

These are all sections of Sugar Daddy profiles posted on SeekingArrangement.com. Each one is different; I could have put in a dozen more and each would be distinct from all the others. The same is true for the women – the Sugar Babies – who come to the website looking for No Strings Attached (NSA) arrangements/relationships.

The stereotype of the filthy-rich old man and the gold-digging girl half his age is utterly outdated. That version of Sugar Babies and Daddies went to the same place, wherever it may be, as the devoted asexual wife in an apron, her workaholic hubby, their two-point-three children, and their station wagon. Over the course of the past twenty or thirty years, virtually every institution and relationship in American society has expanded and altered, largely as a result of the Sexual Revolution and feminism. Why would Sugar relationships be any different? Like everything else, they've changed, and the old stereotypes no longer apply.

The trouble is, nobody seems to have noticed, except for the Sugar lovers who congregate on these kinds of websites. This becomes glaringly obvious each time a newspaper or TV show runs a story on the subject: public outcry from the citizenry is always intense. They equate Sugar arrangements with prostitution, and assume that all Sugar Daddies are committing adultery. The fact is, less than half the men who frequent SeekingArrangement.com are married, and I don't know a single Sugar Baby who feels like a prostitute.

> Just because a woman gets something in exchange doesn't make her a whore; giving it away to someone who cares nothing about her is what makes her cheap. I lived a so-called honorable celibate life for many years (saving myself for Mr. Right) and men just thought I was weird. I would rather have fun and money than sit around being bored and honorable.

That's a post by a Sugar Baby from the SeekingArrangement blog. Notice it doesn't exactly fit the old image of Sugar Babies as superficial, uncaring home wreckers interested in only one thing – money. The reality is, many of the women on SeekingArrangement are over thirty; some are single mothers, others are students or fledgling entrepreneurs. This writer wants help with her career:

> I published my first book a year ago this month. The perfect arrangement for me would be one that provided for my living so I can work less, and write and promote my books more. I like to dress up in sexy dresses or evening gowns just as much as to wear jeans and a tight T-Shirt. I have adult children who live in other states. I love to cook and try new recipes. I can take care of the special needs of that special man extremely well, but we would have to have some chemistry. I don't have a problem making a commitment, if desired.

This Sugar Baby may not even realize it, but what she's looking for is a patron, once quite commonplace in Europe: a wealthy benefactor who supports the arts by assisting individual artists. Hers is just one of scores of reasons that women choose to go the Sugar Baby route. There are even some who don't need money, but are in it for adventure.

I've been a Sugar Baby since I was 22 (now 31). I've stayed in a Milanese palazzo, visited Amsterdam a dozen times, launched my own business, turned down two marriage proposals, had my own marriage proposal rejected, and pretty much bought all the shoes in Saks.

And here's more breaking news: if you think every Sugar Baby wants a male Daddy, you're in for a surprise. Changes in the Sugar Bowl mirror the changes in society: some Sugar Babies are male (both gay and straight), some are lesbians, and some Daddies aren't Daddies at all, they're Mamas.

My nights are free. I need a young puppy to tease and spoil, a male sugar baby who'll hang out and relax with me. Massages, chocolate, candles, oils. In return, I'll help you with rent, school, that sort of thing.

• • • • •

Most people think that a male sugar baby is either weird or impossible, but I am one. I want to be pampered and live like a prince. I admit I'm impatient and expect that a Sugar Mama or Sugar Daddy will just snatch me up right away. In short, I am conceited.

• • • • •

As a gay sugar daddy I've come to believe there's a fine line between desperate and direct. There's nothing wrong with a Sugar Baby expressing his desires or expectations, just as there's nothing wrong with a Sugar Daddy expressing his. But it's how all of it is handled that's key.

Not only is there a wide diversity of people in the Sugar Bowl, but arrangement variations are limited only by one's imagination.

My Sugar Baby is an aspiring model, and all she really wants is someone to travel with her. I take her around to her photo shoots. She earns nice money from the work, while I take care of all travel expenses – four-star hotels, fine restaurants, fun activities. I escort her to photo shoots to make sure everything's safe for her. So far we've gone to New York, Chicago, Phoenix, Seattle, Vancouver, and even London. Both of us are having a blast.

Sugar Images in Pop Culture

These arrangements are doubtless a revelation to most people; that's partly because the Sugar lifestyle is portrayed in pop culture in such hackneyed ways. Like many alternative lifestyles, the Sugar Bowl is grist for the cultural mill, apt to be distorted in books and film. Hollywood hasn't yet caught up to the idea of change: Sugar Babies are painted as ruthless gold-diggers, and Sugar Daddies as lecherous old men preying on the young and innocent. Even in a fairly positive film like Pretty Woman, the partners come together out of desperation: she's desperately poor, he's desperately lonely. Real life is seldom this black and white.

Another picture of a Sugar-type relationship was recently presented in The Other Boleyn Girl, a movie about the historical figures Anne and Mary Boleyn, mistresses to the ultimate Sugar Daddy, the King of England. For their daughters' services the elder Boleyns cash in on royal favors – which is precisely why they arranged the situation. It's all a scandal and a mess, the girls shamelessly mistreated.

Given the sketchy facts available on the true history of the Boleyn girls, a multitude of scenarios might have been created, but Hollywood chose to tell the same old story: helpless young girls exploited by men, their mother powerless to protect them. Sugar King is led around by his dick, with no concern for consequences, not even for his country. Not that such a scenario is inconceivable: think John Edwards.

Ironically, the Sugar concept was treated with more sympathy by Hollywood fifty years ago, with Marilyn Monroe typecast as an ingénue on the hunt for wealth and diamonds. She played this part in Gentlemen Prefer Blondes, How To Marry a Millionaire, and Some Like it Hot (in which even her name was Sugar!). Even in her last movie, The Misfits, she did a variation on Sugar Baby, as a young woman being mentored by an older man (Clark Gable).

Strangely enough, while Hollywood presents Sugar Daddies as predators, slackers get the royal treatment. A well-lit leading man struggles to find himself in a lonely, cold world, daring to buck the system by forging his own path. Meanwhile, today's women complain about this generation of slackers being devoid of ambition. In real life there's no rock n' roll soundtrack, no happy ending, no sidekick for comic relief – and not much in the way of nobility, which vanishes in the pure light of day. As an old Ebb and Kander song put it, "Hearts grow hard on a windy street/Lips grow cold with the rent to meet."

Why wouldn't a young woman prefer a Sugar Daddy? One blogger said she was sick of meeting the kind of guy "who can't call me because he forgot to pay his cell phone bill." Another blogger, fed up with guys her own age, finally registered with SeekingArrangement. "I just want a guy who can give me the finer things in life," she said. "I only live once and I don't want to compromise."

Some of today's Sugar Babies will probably be tomorrow's wives; despite "the best laid plans" for NSA relationships, Sugar Babies and Daddies sometimes fall in love (this is discussed more in Chapter 11). I'd even go so far as to guess that a small percentage of Sugar Babies online have marriage in mind when they first register.

Where else would they find ambitious, successful or soon-to-be successful men, given the predominance of the slacker mentality? A few women have said on the blog that they visit Sugar websites precisely because it's where to find ambitious men. It's a smart woman who goes hunting among the wealthy and creative.

A Cup of Sugar in Every Pantry

Not only are more than half of all Sugar Daddies single—they aren't all fabulously wealthy. When I did a segment on the Playboy radio channel, a truck driver called in to ask if it was possible for him to be a Sugar Daddy. After determining he was making over $75K a year and had two thousand in disposable income per month, I assured him he could indeed afford a Sugar Baby, as long as he had the gift of generosity. Financial attitude is more important in a Sugar Daddy than having a high dollar amount to spend: two thousand is certainly enough for weekly restaurant dinners, gifts of flowers, lingerie and an occasional piece of jewelry, and even a small allowance.

Thus, a man with an average income can indulge himself in what may have been his lifelong fantasy. He can "keep" a gorgeous, young, sweet, sexy, high-quality Sugar Baby without being a multi-millionaire, even in times of economic downturn. The Internet has made it possible for men of comparatively modest means to join the party. On SeekingArrangement, twenty women register for every man, and with those odds, someone's bound to be attracted to our trucker friend.

As I said in the introduction, SeekingArrangement and other niche websites have leveled the playing field. By engaging in sugar relationships, the ordinary man who once had to compete for the attention of beautiful girls can finally stand out of the crowd and indulge in intimacy with lovely Sugar Babies.

The Shiny New Sugar Bowl

If the old definitions no longer suffice to describe the reality of these relationships, we need to create new definitions, expanding them to include the diversity of types in the Sugar community. What exactly is a Sugar Daddy/ Sugar Baby/ Sugar Mama?

Perhaps it will help to first look at the qualities that are universally common in Sugar relationships, no matter who the people or what their motivations. A few essential qualities are endemic to an arranged, NSA, Sugar-inspired relationship:

- the experience of pleasure, usually but not always including the physical;
- the free expression and satisfaction of both partners' needs and desires;
- opportunities and enthusiasm for fun;
- mutually beneficial rewards.

The first three are self-explanatory, while the fourth, mutually beneficial rewards, requires some explication. Not surprisingly, this is an area in which traditional relationships often run into trouble. It separates the traditional from the sweet, in that each one holds a radically different perspective.

In traditional relationships, supposedly forged of love and love alone, to openly acknowledge an exchange of one thing for another is seen as calculating. Marriage proposals aren't usually made with "mutually beneficial rewards" in mind, at least not consciously. A man and woman on the verge of lifetime commitment seldom tell each other what they want to gain for themselves – to do so would be considered horribly selfish. Nowadays pre-nuptial agreements are common – but these only spell out what's going to happen if the couple splits. Odd, isn't it, that a couple would be so cautious as to draw up a contract for an eventuality that might not come to pass – and yet never even talk about, much less write down, what they want to occur during the course of the actual relationship.

This is where Sugar relationships make a radical departure from tradition: by the second date, if things are going well, Sugar Babies and Daddies are talking about how often they want to see one another, whether or not they'll be monogamous, how much cash, if any, he'll give her, and other terms of their arrangement. Of course, this is the ideal Sugar process; in actual practice, some people shy away from raising these issues, or for other reasons just never get around to them. For the sake of argument, however, let's use the ideal as the norm. At the very least, it's what Sugar Babies and Daddies strive for.

What's considered ideal to Sugar Babies and Daddies is anathema to traditionalists. Stating one's needs is thought of as selfish, ungenerous, grabby, and unromantic, particularly if one of those needs is financial. To most conventional citizens, any time money enters the picture it's prostitution, plain and simple. You can read this in tirades responding to online articles about Sugar relationships; readers express outrage on behalf of Sugar Babies, who they see as victims. But do Sugar Babies themselves feel like victims? Straight from the horse's mouth:

> So many women let themselves be used casually for nothing. After being in a couple of relationships in which my boyfriends did nothing but take, and were never around when I needed them, I have chosen the SB route because at least it's up front, and men have no excuse not to spoil me a little. When you date a man in a traditional way, he usually wants something casual where you sleep with him and go out with him, but you live apart and pay your own bills and even split the check at dinner. I have no interest in that kind of relationship. If I'm in a casual relationship with no future, I want to savor the moment and have something to show for it – or at least build up my wardrobe.

No matter how many times Sugar Babies say they're comfortable with the role and the lifestyle, they continue to be judged. It bothers people to no end to hear that some partners consciously negotiate for what they want. Even when money isn't involved, they consider negotiating "cold." Ironically, it's this promise of mutual benefits and rewards that's the main attraction to many Sugar Babies. Most of them, as well as Sugar Mamas and Daddies, spent a good deal of time figuring out what they wanted before jumping into the Sugar Bowl. They aren't settling for an arrangement after all else fails – they're choosing the land of Sugar because it's where they want to be.

> I like to think of myself as a modern-day geisha with a different perspective on an honest relationship. Many times in the process of trying to find love we look for red flags and annoying habits in a person. In a Sugar Daddy/Sugar Baby relationship, those things don't matter. If he leaves the toothpaste cap off, it's not a problem, because he goes home. If he doesn't like the fact that I don't make the bed every day, no worries: he has his own place. The relationship becomes all about pleasing and being pleased.

This Sugar Baby obviously chose the lifestyle because she prefers the greater emotional independence it allows.

Now that we've delineated the commonalities in Sugar relationships, we can come to new definitions of Sugar Babies and Sugar Daddies.

Sugar Daddy – A man who provides financial, professional, or other forms of support to an individual in exchange for personal benefit (e.g., intimacy, companionship, etc.).

Sugar Mama – A woman who provides financial, professional, or other forms of support to an individual in exchange for personal benefit (e.g., intimacy, companionship, etc.).

Sugar Baby – An individual who provides intimacy, companionship, or other forms of attention in exchange for personal benefit (e.g., financial support, professional advancement, etc.).

If one person finds happiness in one kind of relationship, it doesn't mean someone else can't find it in another. There ought to be room in this world for all kinds of relationships, including Sugar Daddy/ Sugar Baby arrangements.

the New Arranged Relationship

CHAPTER TWO:

WHAT'S LOVE GOT TO DO WITH IT?

What's love got to do, got to do with it?
What's love but a second hand emotion?
—Tina Turner

"*What's Love Got to Do with It?*" was the first big hit Tina Turner recorded solo, after leaving Ike, her abusive husband and musical mentor. Everyone knew the story, and millions of women all over the world applauded the song, a declaration of independence:

independence from what we call *love*. (In Tina's case, as in far too many, *love* was a form of slavery.) It was a revolutionary song that could be interpreted on several levels. First, it made a distinction between love and sex, something that women have always found difficult to do. On another level, the song strongly suggested we don't *have* to be in love in order to enjoy sexual pleasure. This was a radical message indeed.

Some people, of course, frown on that message; they're quick to judge any relationship that deviates from the cultural norm. They seem to understand the forces that keep a woman in an abusive marriage, and are tolerant of other, less-than-perfect ones. But they can't extend the same understanding to someone who gets involved in anything the least bit "kinky." Disapproval of Sugar Daddy/Sugar Baby relationships comes from the same mindset as disapproval of polyamory, or open marriage…pretty much any configuration outside conventional norms. Those who practice different lifestyles get labeled deviant, sneaky, or immoral. The majority of the population believes that relationships should always be based on True Love, notions of My One and Only, and Happily Ever After.

Now, I'm not going to tell you there's no such thing as True Love, or that nobody was ever happy being with one steady mate forever and ever. The problem is that we've been told this is the natural order of the universe, that it happens almost by magic – but in truth, it takes a lot of hard work to maintain a successful relationship. The belief in magical fairytale love probably does more to damage real live relationships than mid-life crises, cheating, or financial problems all combined. That's because in real life, relationships seldom live up to the unattainable fantasy. Dreams die hard. When the cherished dream of Romantic Love comes crashing down, disappointed lovers direct their bitterness at each other. The individuals get blamed rather than the setup, with its built-in potential for implosion.

Does any of this make sense?

Mother Nature, Evolution and Biology

Most of us are so indoctrinated with the myth of Romantic Love that we automatically assume it's the driving force behind every twosome. Meanwhile, Mother Nature must surely be laughing at our ignorance – *we* might think of love as natural, but the only thing *she* gives a damn about is reproduction. She adorns sex with romantic frills so we'll do what she wants us to: *be fruitful and multiply.* It's called *the reproductive imperative,* and it compelled the first caveman to haul the first cavewoman into his humble abode.

Not too long after Tina Turner asked what love had in common with a knee-jerk chemical reaction, scientists began asking the same question. Their research is leading them to believe that our choices are driven more by Mother Nature's hormonal elixirs than by love, romantic or otherwise.

One of the things research uncovered is that the way we feel when "in love" actually *is* more chemical than romantic. During the early stages of love – or *limerence* in evolutionary biology lingo – the brain is flooded with endorphins, those hormones that also get fired up by jumping around to music. Endorphins suffuse the body with a sense of almost blissful well-being. This condition is not unlike being drugged, and it can last as long as three years – just the right length of time for two people to meet, get to know each other, form an ongoing sexual relationship, and start thinking babies. This suits

Mother Nature just fine. But unless you and your lover are dedicated marathon runners, the endorphins eventually wear off. What's left of a relationship once those endorphins fall back to normal levels? If a couple is lucky, they've managed to find enough commonalities during the limerence phase to cement their relationship. But if they came together solely out of physical attraction, the momentum's bound to slow down, like the bat of a baseball slugger whose home-run stats drop precipitously when they take away his steroids.

These new scientific enquiries were spurred by an expanding field of study called evolutionary biology, popularized in the 1990's by several best-selling books, including Anatomy of Love: The Natural History of Monogamy, Adultery, and Divorce, by Helen E. Fisher, and Sexual Strategies: How Females Choose Their Mates, by Mary Batten. Evolutionary biology rests on the theory that all human behavior is aimed at perpetuating the race. Just like every other species, from ants to elephants, we've been programmed to survive not just as individuals, but as a species; in fact, group survival is more important to Mother Nature than individual lives.

This message runs through the ages and across all cultures and species. Evolutionary biology takes the long view, with a perspective that allows us to relax and stop beating ourselves up for our human foibles: they probably evolved in order to serve the reproductive imperative. Even adultery may have been practiced in the service of that imperative: as the theory goes, prehistoric men were spreading their sperm around to produce as many offspring as possible, while promiscuous females were busily confusing the question of paternity so as to ensure a pool of potential fathers would help raise the kids.

Contemporary readers are no doubt laughing, thinking we are

eons removed from these primitive behaviors. Think again: the criteria by which primitive lovers chose one another isn't so different from the way mates make choices in the Sugar Bowl. When the world was young and sparsely populated, women were more active in mate selection, and they invariably crawled into the bushes with the male who was most successful. Male success was measured by hunting ability and signs of physiological virility. When men did the choosing, they went for the most physically attractive women and those with wide, sturdy hips good for breeding.

How are mates chosen in the Sugar Bowl? Daddies are chosen for their success, measured by the ability to scare up money instead of meat. A Sugar Baby is still chosen for her good looks (though I'm at a loss to explain the modern preference for slim-hipped women). Even though the planet no longer needs to be populated, early programming still influences our behavior.

This is actually cause for celebration: it's comforting to know we're in touch with Mother Nature, and it gives us a broader life view: our own time and place, with all its attendant psychological *angst,* is not the only way of life humankind has ever known. We are, as Joni Mitchell said, *billion-year-old carbons,* with ancestors before us and, if we don't blow it, progeny after. In the context of a grand evolutionary process, our petty and even not-so-petty mating problems shrink to more manageable proportions.

Arrangements and Arranged Marriage

The practice of arranged marriage, still common in places like India and China, actually bears some similarity to Sugar arrangements. It too comes under fire from romance junkies who suspect any coupling not born of spontaneous love combustion. Again, arranged marriages have been going on for so long that if we open our minds to it, we'll find our worldview broadened. Unfortunately, no accurate statistics exist as to the success of arranged versus love marriages; the divorce rate is lower among those that are arranged, but it is believed to be because divorce is taboo among those cultures.

Not every society throughout time and history based the institution of marriage on a fleeting emotion. Proponents of romantic love feel superior to these ancient traditions, and they pity the "poor kids" whose parents "force" them to marry a "stranger." If people would just do some homework, they'd discover that many traditional arrangements are carefully thought out. Parents gather tons of data on potential mates for their children, and conscientiously try to ensure the best possible match, keeping their children's future happiness in mind.

Among Cambodian Buddhists, it is considered a sacred duty for parents to marry off their children to good families. The children are expected to demonstrate their gratitude to them for finding suitable partners by fulfilling their marital obligations.

In Western society people fall in love before they wed; in arranged marriage, there is also love, but it usually happens afterwards, over time, as spouses grow to love one another. This is frequently anticipated. The partners came together for a purpose, usually to create a family; this kind of marriage can have at least as solid a foundation, if not more so, than one based on feelings of the moment.

This isn't always the case, of course. Different cultures have different traditions – for instance, among the old European royals, girls were often betrothed as children, with no choice whatsoever in the matter. In some Hindu sects, a girl becomes a widow if her betrothed dies before she grows up, and she's then doomed to an empty, cloistered life. Horror stories abound of mismatches, brutal husbands, unfaithful wives and their punishments. But the same can be said of marriages based on romantic love, or on any other criteria. Human beings are complicated creatures – how can our intimate relationships be anything less?

Sugar relationships, like traditional arranged marriages, require research; in both systems, potential partners are pre-screened and exhaustively interviewed; both are based on specific mutual needs; and both can lead to genuine love. The only significant difference is that in traditional marriage it's the parents who do the negotiating rather than the individuals themselves. While exactly what's negotiated *for* might be very different, the process is much the same.

Sugar Baby Lineage

Almost nothing is new under the sun. Even Sugar Babies have a long and distinguished lineage.

In ancient Greece, *hetaerae* were independent women who were required to dress in distinctive garb. Mostly ex-slaves and foreigners, they were courtesans renowned for achievement in dance and music, as well as the sensual arts. They seem to have been regarded as distinct from *pornê* or simple prostitutes, but were also distinguished from mistresses or wives. Unlike most women in Greek society, they were educated and paid taxes. They were the only women who took part in the symposia, where their opinions were respected. *Hetaerae* were highly prized for their intellect, especially their conversational skills (as well as other, ahem, *gifts*). They were sought after, and enjoyed a great deal of power and influence.

These were not the first, or last, Sugar Babies in history. The *Nadītu* in early Babylon, the Japanese *Oiran*, and the Korean *kisaeng* were all complex figures whose position in their respective societies fell somewhere between entertainers and prostitutes.

The Japanese *Geisha* evolved from the *Oiran*. Because the latter were highly paid courtesans, there remains some confusion, even in Japan, as to the *Geisha's* duties. While frequently depicted in Western pop culture as expensive prostitutes, *Geisha* are strictly entertainers; they do not engage in paid sex. Even though a Geisha's repertoire might include flirting and playful innuendo, her clients expect nothing more – and they seem to be sufficiently amused by the mere illusion of sexual pleasure.

In nineteenth century Europe the *demimonde* was a polite term equivalent to the Western *mistress*. It referred to a class of women on the fringes of respectable society who were supported by wealthy lovers; most *demimonde* had several. Smart *demimonde*, like the fictional *Gigi's* grandmother, invested their wealth for the day when their beauty would fade.

The *demimonde* were common among the upper classes of French, English and even American society, and the term broadened to describe an entire social class. It comes from the French for "half-world," implying that they lived on the fringes of society – and yet they enjoyed an extravagant lifestyle of fine food and clothes, surpassing that of most other wealthy women of their day, because of the steady income from multiple lovers. Like the Greek *hetaerae*, the *demimondes'* wit, beauty and intellect kept them from a lesser fate. Some presided over salons considered "disreputable," while at the same time they were widely celebrated.

They sure sound like Sugar Babes to me.

Who would've known that today's Sugar Babies have such a long and respected lineage? It ought to make them proud to know they're part of an ongoing historical tradition.

If This Isn't Love…

Love is still a mysterious, not always controllable force – and who would want it any other way? Despite the determination of the most unromantic Sugar Daddy, or the efforts of the most cautious Sugar Baby, sometimes they fall in love.

> I currently live in San Diego with my SD of eight months. I'm not in love, but that's something I work very hard not to do. In a Sugar Daddy relationship, the "love" word isn't something to get too familiar with.
>
> • • • • •
>
> I had an amazing arrangement with an SD from this site. I just got out of a long marriage and was not and am not looking for anything serious, so I put very specifically in my profile that if you want your soul mate or a whole future, please pass me by. My SD was perfect, with an allowance, gifts and connection. We had a blast, in many different places. He became very attached to me, though, and I felt our adventure as SD/SB should end. We remain friends but do not see each other. He will probably always be a good friend in my life, but I just don't want anything serious.

As evidenced by the above, Sugar relationships, begun strictly with *No Strings Attached,* can lead to genuine love. How the people involved handle it depends on who they are and the circumstances of their lives. One Sugar Baby seems to be fairly comfortable with it.

> I think it is all about love, but not in the traditional sense....it's what makes you happy to wake up and find out what'll happen today; it's always wanting to take a few extra minutes in the mirror...just in case; or thinking of everything he said, so you can figure out a new way to make him smile.

One Sugar Daddy summed it up wisely.

> Love is dangerous within a no-strings-attached intention, but too exciting to pass up. Lives change when love brings you back to yourself.

Still, falling in love to the point of wanting to change the arrangement to a conventional one seems to be the exception rather than the rule. The goal of a majority of Sugar relationships remains the same: to have a good time together, to help one another out as originally negotiated, and to serve as an oasis of calm amid life's inevitable stresses. We'll talk more about overdose – or falling in love with a Sugar mate – in Chapter 11.

"Good Father by day… Bad Daddy by night."

CHAPTER THREE:

WHAT'S SEX GOT TO DO WITH IT?

"Sex is a part of nature, I go along with nature."
—*Marilyn Monroe*

Sex is a part of every dating experience, from blind dates to speed dating to bar pickups. It's even present, if covertly, on Christian dating websites – do you think the guys go there for friendship only? Most women aren't quite as preoccupied as men are with sex, but be assured, they also think about it, and more than most people suspect – particularly during more active periods of dating. The mere act of posting a profile online brings sex to the front and center of the mind, so every time a woman makes a date, and during the days leading up to it, she'll wonder if they're going to end up in the bedroom – even if she swears to herself she won't. On any first date, both genders drift in and out of preoccupation with the questions *Do I want to sleep with him/her?* and *Do I want to do it tonight?* While a few Sugar Babies, and some Sugar Daddies, are looking for companionship only, without the sexual component (we'll talk about those later), almost everyone else doing online dating has sex on the brain – and in a few other body parts as well!

If It Looks Like A Duck and Quacks Like a Duck...
...it isn't always a duck. Really.

When people first hear about Sugar arrangements, they invariably jump to the conclusion that it's prostitution – an utterly false assumption. Several factors separate the sugar from the trade. To begin with, prostitution happens when one person offers his or her body for a specified period of time to another person, in exchange for a specified amount of cash. In a Sugar relationship, two equal people negotiate terms of agreement, some about sex, some about money, and some about any number and variety of issues. There is much more to a Sugar Daddy/Baby relationship than sex.

> Anyone who thinks that what we're talking about here is simply quid pro quo, cash for sex, is mistaken. That's not a relationship, that's an escort on a retainer.

Nothing wrong with that, but it's not what I'm personally looking for and not what this is all about. In a true SD/SB relationship, many gifts are offered from each side, some of them intangible.

—A Sugar Baby on the SeekingArrangement blog

Another assumption people make is that, since Sugar Daddies tend to be older, Sugar Babies don't find them attractive, so sex is just part of the job for her. In reality, not all Sugar Daddies are ancient, and Sugar Babies are frequently just as enthusiastic, and get just as much pleasure out of sex.

My requirements are fabulous shoes and rip-roarin' sex – and I managed to find both in one wonderful Sugar Daddy.

Not only is this Sugar Baby in it for the sex, but her Sugar Daddy's age apparently doesn't interfere with his ability to fulfill her "requirements".

Maybe Sugar Daddies used to be strictly old, but that's another thing that's changed in our world: these days more young men have disposable income than in generations past. On SeekingArrangment. com a fairly large number of men are in their 30s and 40s. Some are trust fund babies, others struck it rich early in life. The dot-com world is rife with young millionaires.

Even if a man is older, it doesn't mean he can't enjoy a full sex life – that's just another outdated stereotype. In *Still Doing It*, a collection of personal stories, men and women in their 60s, 70s and yes, even their 80s, describe having active sex lives – and that's pre-Viagra! Today, with chemical assistance, a guy can get it up and keep it up.

Up or not, an older man sometimes does better in bed than a young stud; more than one Sugar Baby says she prefers the over-forty set. An older man isn't in a hurry; he doesn't come fast, and he takes his time pleasing a woman. As the Pointer Sisters sang:

I want a man with a slow hand
I want a lover with an easy touch
I want somebody who will spend some time
Not come and go in a heated rush.

An older man's been around the block a few times, so by now he's learned a thing or two about female psychology and anatomy. He's not too shy to talk about sex either – and, as everyone knows, communication is the Number One sex enhancement technique. By virtue of having lived longer, and having had more experience, older men communicate with greater ease than younger ones.

I'm generalizing, of course – plenty of guys somehow manage to bumble through three or four marriages without learning a thing about women or how to talk to them. Inept oafs exist at every age and economic level. Still, all other things being equal, it's the guy with a few notches in his belt that's going to do better between the sheets.

Besides, if a particular Sugar Daddy happens to be inept, Sugar Baby doesn't have to rely on him alone to satisfy her. It all depends on their agreement as to whether she's free to see and sleep with other men when Daddy's not around. He'll probably want to be her first priority – but Daddies are wealthy, and wealthy men are busy, and busy men don't hang out with one woman 24/7.

This is one of those topics that should be discussed during the negotiating phase of an arrangement. If you want to have other lovers, be clear and up front about it. Don't just assume non-monogamy; some Sugar Daddies do prefer a one-man woman.

Ultimately it's up to each individual Sugar Baby and Sugar Daddy to decide what they can or will accept in this area. Needless to say, if she's not a monogamous mistress and/or he's not a faithful Daddy, they should practice safe sex.

The Greatest Aphrodisiac

Every type of sexual relationship tends to have its own built-in erotic elements, and Sugar affairs are no exception. Inherent in Sugar love is the eroticism of power. Someone (I think it was Henry Kissinger) once said that power is the greatest aphrodisiac of all. In a world where money equals power, it's not unusual for lavish spending to trigger an erotic response.

The sex industry, in which men pay to see, hear, touch, and fuck women, is one obvious place where sex is blatantly exchanged for money. But if you know how to decode messages, the concept is all around us. Ask any woman if she's ever fantasized about being a stripper or porno star, and the answer will undoubtedly be yes. In *Three Tall Women*, a play by Edward Albee, an old lady tells a younger one that her husband once draped a pearl necklace over his naked cock and told her if she wanted the jewels she had to get them off with her mouth. Even those stalwarts of convention, the women's magazines, advise wives to spice up their marriages by occasionally playing the tart.

Sex in exchange for money gets played out in all kinds of subtle ways, including – even especially – within the marital structure. Those good citizens who label Sugar Babies prostitutes, and wives virtuous, will no doubt be stunned by this point of view, but the reality of Hubby sweating off his balls to care for Wifey-poo, who cooks and cleans and polishes his shoes, is precisely what keeps a lot of couples fucking like bunnies, even if they've come to despise one another.

> "I have too many fantasies to be a housewife. I guess I am a fantasy."
>
> —*Marilyn Monroe*

The scent of sex for money even permeates the work place. We hear a lot these days about powerful female CEOs, but most women are still far more likely to work as waitresses or secretaries. *The Playboy Club* bunny was[1] the most un-subtle example: a pretty little pet who scurried about fetching drinks and food for an all-male clientele. They weren't being paid just for food service – any robot can do that – but for keeping their customers hard and happy. While some of this has changed thanks to sexual harassment laws, waitresses still flirt for bigger tips. And let's not forget *Hooters!*

Whether it's obvious or not, the male/female money/power dynamic permeates our collective consciousness, and it's not going to die out so easily, no matter how many women become VPs – of corporations or the country.

The Eroticism of Daddy

Another element that spins Sugar into hot pink candy is the whole concept of Daddy. Women's sexual fantasies – based, I admit, on anecdotal evidence, but a lot of it – frequently revolve around a Daddy figure. I don't mean their actual fathers, but the idea of an authority figure who doles out punishment, yet at the same time loves and protects her. Women don't see themselves as children in this fanta-

1 The first Playboy Club in 25 years, complete with bunnies, opened in Las Vegas in 2006.

sy – indeed, the mentality here is ageless – but as being "powerless", at the mercy of a powerful man.

Daddy carries an enormous weight on his strong shoulders: after all, women have been repeatedly told that their fathers influence their sexual development, and that they tend to fall in love with men who remind them of him. Thus, sex with a Daddy figure is fraught with Freudian overtones, shrouded in secrecy, and tinged with taboos. It doesn't *get* any hotter than this!

One common root of the Daddy fantasy is the desire for a lover who's super loyal and will never leave, no matter what. There's a scene in *The Misfits* in which Marilyn Monroe cries uncontrollably when Clark Gable, her older lover/mentor, gets mad and yells at her. Sobbing, she asks him if he still likes her.

"Come on, honey," he says, pulling her into his big bear arms, "Didn't your Papa ever spank you, then pick you up and give you a big kiss? He did, didn't he?"

"He was never there long enough," Marilyn cries. "Strangers spanked me for keeps." She collapses into Gable's arms, the quintessential little girl, comforted by the archetypal Daddy. She is at once a vulnerable child and a powerfully erotic adult woman. When she yields to the force of Gable's masculinity, she gives up her power, something that Monroe did repeatedly with her leading men. While some thought of Marilyn as a victim, in reality she was so powerful, and *so aware of her power*, that she was able to surrender it without fear of losing it completely.

Here's a real kicker: the Daddy fantasy is not confined to women only. *Doing it for Daddy* is an anthology consisting entirely of gay male sex stories. For years the personal ads in gay men's magazines have expressed wanting father/son sexual relationships. On the SeekingArrangement site, male Sugar Babies seek Sugar Daddies, and vice versa. If even men have these fantasies, surely there is something inherently erotic about Daddy.

> Amazing body, great looks. Looking to be that "trophy boy" that every man wants, but only wealthy men can afford. Looking to please my daddy in every way imaginable. Not looking for a part time arrangement, but for the real deal. I want to be a "kept boy" and make all of daddy's friends jealous.

The logical question arises, why is Mommy so rarely conjured up for the same purpose? The simple answer is, in our culture, Mommies don't have erotic power. Like everything else, though, this is slowly changing, and it will grow and evolve as women continue to gain economic power. The few Sugar Mamas on the site want the same kinds of arrangements as Daddies. Interestingly, Mamas tend to be fairly explicit in their profiles:

> Hot Mama seeking Boy Toy: Are you a boy toy looking for fun? Are you well-equipped too? Let's see what you've got, big boy, and we'll have some fun!

· · · · ·

> I'm separated from my husband and will soon be divorced. I'm looking for a male or female Sugar Baby to go on business trips and spend special weekends alone with me at my Cape Cod home. Must be young and have a sense of style.

Sugar Mamas are the most sought after group on SeekingArrangement.com. That's because the ratio is one Mama for approximately 200 male, and lesbian, Sugar Babies. This is primarily due to women's current lower economic status, a demographic that's in a state of constant change. (We'll go into more about Sugar Mamas in a later chapter.) Thus, every Sugar Mama is in a position of power: she can have her pick of the litter, so to speak. Talk about leveling the playing field! Not only do Sugar relationships benefit the economically average man, they also open up opportunities for women you don't find in some other areas of life.

Negotiating Sex in the Sugar Bowl

I have a friend who says he sometimes forgets to eat, and then when he gets hungry he thinks he's horny. I don't know any women who confuse hunger with horniness, do you? There's just no getting around it: men have sex on the brain 24/7. This has a profound effect on the negotiating of sex in arrangements.

Sugar Daddy's ready to raise the subject of sex immediately, and sometimes does in the first email. Some Sugar Daddies consider themselves restrained if they wait until the first date to bring it up! Meanwhile, Sugar Baby's bitin' her bones to keep from raising the money subject, and gets turned off when all he talks about is sex, sex, sex.

Listen up, guys, and listen good: It's a safe bet that a woman brave and bold enough to post a profile on SeekingArrangement is no wilting wallflower, certainly not a stranger to sex. She wants it. She might even want it just as much as you do, but (a) she was raised not to admit it; (b) she feels used if that's all you talk about; and (c) she's conflicted about jumping into bed right away.

Keep listening – only now listen to what Sugar Babies themselves have to say.

So many of the guys on this site put too much about sex in their profile. They lack class. I have come across some that are into depraved sexual practices that wouldn't make any woman feel like a Sugar Baby. A lot of these guys want to get sexual right away, so there's no time to develop a fondness for them beyond what they look like.

• • • • •

I was planning on meeting with a gentleman today for the first time, but was disappointed when he suggested getting a hotel room and having "adult fun". I am not on this site as a prostitute.

• • • • •

He said, "I think what I would like to do is have you stay the night and see what we think." Uh, shame on me if I'm jumping to conclusions, but that sounded like "how about you come over one night and we have sex and we can go from there." I don't want the first time I meet him to be at his home, at night.

• • • • •

Numerous SDs have requested nude pictures of me within the first or second contact. I was very disappointed when I finally found someone in my little town, and the first thing he asks for is nude pics!

Sugar Daddies: Maybe it makes you angry that women won't address sex immediately. Maybe you think it's hypocritical, and resent having to pussyfoot around her "delicate sensibilities." Even so, you might as well get over it, and accept the way things are. Why? Because *it is the way things are.* Thousands of years of conditioning by society, or Mother Nature, or just plain Mother, are not going to be bypassed in the next few months or years or decades – so if you really want to be successful in relationships, the best thing you can do is learn how to deal with the aforesaid way things are. Here are a few general guidelines:

- *Don't raise the subject of sex in email unless she does.*
- *Don't raise it on the first, second or third date, unless she does.*

Exception: If she raises the subject of money in a specific way, then it's acceptable for you to raise the subject of sex. The following is an exchange between a Sugar Baby and Daddy on the blog:

I always wait for him to mention money, unless he gets very specific about the sex. Honestly, for me it's not all about the money (although it is a necessary component), and I hope that for him it isn't all about the sex. I think when it's strictly about sex and money, that's when it's prostitution.

• • • • •

If he talks sex, you can talk money...absolutely, in my opinion, and I'm starting to think the reverse should be true. If she talks money, he can then talk sex. I'd prefer it to be out of the equation entirely until you get to know each other in person.

• *When you do get around to talking sex,* **don't** *be crude.* **Do** *be flirty, playful, somewhat romantic, and appreciative of her sexiness. If you don't know the difference, then:*

• **Do** *pay attention to her reactions for cues. If she's tongue-tied, or looking tense, or red in the face, then you're probably not in sync with her sensibilities. On the other hand, if she's genuinely smiling or laughing, or responding verbally or with body language and gestures, you're probably on the right track.*

• **Don't** *expect sex every single time you meet, even after the ice has been broken.*

• **Do** *talk about sex in a natural kind of way after establishing a sexual relationship. Here's where the male propensity for sex talk comes in handy: when sexual issues need discussing, you can bring them up, sparing her the agony. On the other hand, if she's perfectly comfortable raising sexual issues – and on this level, many women are – respond positively.* **Don't** *discourage her.*

Kinky Sugar

> I met a guy here that lives close by. His expectations weren't too bad, and it seemed like a reasonable deal. Then he wanted me to get on a webcam to prove I'm the same girl as on my profile. I've never been on a webcam, but I did it. He was pleased that I looked like my profile. Then he asked me to give him a show to prove I'm not shy. Ewwwww. I told him I'm not the girl he's looking for, that I respect myself too much to do that for a complete stranger.

Did this guy have a thing for strippers, or was he just trying to grab whatever he could get without spending a dime? The Yiddish language has a wonderfully descriptive word for this type of person: *shnorer* (mooch in English). Whatever his motives, this guy was way out of bounds.

When it comes to kinks and fetishes – and I don't think most men realize this – women don't get attached to specific, "boutique" sex acts as much as men. The gals on the blog laugh about oddball requests from Sugar Daddies. I suspect that when a Daddy talks about unusual sex acts early in an arrangement – like during negotiations – that's about all he can expect to get, a laugh. I can see why a man would think that the time to bring up the subject of fetishes is during negotiations, but the problem is that people who are unfamiliar with that sort of thing – which is most of the population – are made nervous by it. As in all relationships, there's a time and a place for everything, and the time and place to talk about fetishes within the context of a Sugar arrangement is later – much, much later.

Think about it: Someone is just getting to know you, to find out what makes you tick. She's wondering if you like to travel, or if you'll go traveling together; she's wondering if you cuddle after sex, or if you like to snuggle on the couch watching movies, maybe even porno movies – and then you ask her what her shoe size is, because, you blurt, you worship female feet, the bigger the better. I'm sorry, buddy, but nine women out of ten are going to be alarmed. She'll think you're weird, a pervert. But six months later, when you're making out on her sofa, and you run your hand down her smooth calf, take her foot in your hand and squeeze, then kiss your way down to her toes and start sucking them – *then* she'll find it delightful!

In our culture, unusual sex acts are suspect, and frequently equated with violence. Pay attention the next time a movie character asks his girlfriend to dress up in leather – chances are he'll turn out to be evil, crazy, or both. Fortunately, the kind of woman who'd sign onto a site like SeekingArrangement is already a few steps ahead of average, and she's not apt to be scared off so easily. One adventuresome Sugar Baby listed her collection of sex toys:

> ...under-the-bed restraints by Spotsheets, velcro and canvas restraints for either ankle, wrists or both, and they go under your mattress so if you use both ankle and wrist restraints it basically leaves you spread-eagled... the love swing, the doggie strap, and the sex sling are all very good products if I do say so myself.

Sounds like she's ready for any contingency! She's apparently familiar with bondage lite, as they call it. That particular kind of sex – dominance and submission, with bondage – has become fairly popular over the past decade. Still, proceed with caution even in this area: when a newly met man starts telling a woman he wants to tie her to the bedposts, it's only natural that she'd worry about being hurt. Bondage, lite or otherwise, requires trust – and trust doesn't happen overnight.

There are exceptions, of course; there are always exceptions. Women who've had some experience with dominance/submission and understand it's a game without serious intent might be open to it (or they might hate it). One Sugar Baby was nonchalant.

> Being dominant doesn't bother me at all. If a guy wants me to spank him, make him wear ladies' un-derwear, or use him as a footstool, I really don't have a problem with that.

You should assume, however, that a woman isn't experienced unless and until she offers that information.

There is one fetish that most Sugar Babies are wildly enthusiastic about: shopping. Going shopping with a Daddy who sits outside the dressing room, watches her try on clothes or shoes, and buys her whatever she wants, is a major enjoyment of Sugar Babies. I'm not sure this qualifies as a fetish exactly, but if looked at as if Sugar Daddy's dressing her up like a doll, then I think it does. While little girls got to dress up dolls and dress themselves in costume, most boys were, at the very least, discouraged from doing so. And some of them wanted to. So it's possible that a Shopping Daddy is acting out a fetish with its roots in childhood, which is where most fetishes originate. Whatever it is, she loves it – so go ahead and go to town: dress up your Sugar Baby doll to your heart's content!

What?! No Sex?!

It might sound shocking, but quite a few Sugar Daddies don't even *want* sex to be part of the arrangement; some involve very little sex, or even none at all.

> I'm a 55-year-old CEO, generous to a fault, seeking
> a beautiful woman 21 to 33 to accompany me to the
> theater, black-tie events, business trips. Also into
> quiet dinners, good conversation or just snuggling
> on the sofa watching videos. Sex, no; sensuality, yes.
> Will provide financial assistance as needed to the
> right girl.

While no-sex arrangements certainly aren't the only kind in the Sugar pantheon, they're not as rare as one might expect. Whether the relationship includes sex or not, money isn't always the only or prime motivation for Sugar Babies.

> I'm not in it for the money. I would like to meet a man
> who not only enjoys the finer things in life but every-
> thing that life has to offer. Someone who can sleep in
> a five-star hotel one night and in a sleeping bag in the
> woods the next. Someone who wants to have all kinds of
> fun and adventures with me.
>
> • • • • •
>
> From a Sugar Daddy viewpoint, I believe what we SD's
> are looking for is intimacy. Bottom line. Whether that be
> sexual, confidante, friendship, travel partner. Whatever.
> It is that intimacy that you have with someone who is fa-
> miliar, not just a stranger. If it were solely about the sex,
> well, there are easier and, quite frankly, cheaper means
> to get my needs fulfilled without having to jump thru the
> hoops here on the site. Open a phone book, go online,
> and within an hour that's taken care of. What a SD wants
> is to be with someone familiar, someone with whom they
> are comfortable.

It's interesting that so many of the issues that arise in Sugar relationships echo those in traditional marriage, especially the constant theme of *He wants sex, She wants money.*

One Sugar Baby summed up the Sugar phenomenon beautifully.

> Marriage can be seen as a business arrangement, just like prostitution is a business exchange. We hold marriage on such a high pedestal in society, but it's only successful when both parties want to be there. That's one reason why both men and women are looking for arrangement situations – marriage just isn't as appetizing as it used to be.

We'd been speculating as to why these arrangements are becoming so popular, besides the obvious fact that the Internet makes it possible. She pointed out that in the past, women couldn't support themselves and really needed marriage, while men couldn't find sex so easily outside marriage. Now that those reasons no longer apply so stringently, people only get married if they really want to, primarily for love, while more and more people are choosing other lifestyles.

CHAPTER FOUR:

THE MONEY COMPONENT

She works hard for the money
So hard for it, honey
She works hard for the money
So you better treat her right
—Donna Summer

The video of the old Donna Summer disco tune *She Works Hard for the Money* is a lot more serious than one would expect either from Donna or disco. It follows a single mother through a day in her life of two jobs and two kids. She starts out at the diner, doing the back-breaking work of waitressing; cheerful and peppy, she becomes more weary and hassled as the day goes on. Then she's sitting at a sewing machine in a roomful of other sewing women, struggling to stay awake and do her work. Finally, she trudges home, lugging groceries, to cook for and feed her two rambunctious kids. The ending makes an attempt to inspire, with our hard-working gal dancing in the street among a bunch of other men and women dressed in various kinds of work uniforms.

This is a fairly accurate picture of the life of a single mother. Next time someone expresses disapproval about women who prefer prostitution – or stripping or lap dancing or phone sex – to "work," remind them of this. Same thing goes the next time someone disses a Sugar Baby who prefers her Sugar Daddy to a boss.

It's completely understandable for a savvy woman, whether she has kids or not, to choose the life of a Sugar Baby. As pointed out elsewhere, we hear a lot about female CEOs, when the truth is that waitressing, factory work, and office jobs are what's available to the majority of women. And even CEOs and professional women still earn only seventy-seven cents to every dollar earned by a man. But hey, things are looking up – in 1970 it was only *fifty-one* cents!

> I have an SD I've been seeing for six months. Within the first two months he gave me a $10k check. I didn't even ask for it and we hadn't even had sex yet! Next month I asked for some spending money and he gave me a check for $2k. I wasn't sure if I was asking too much of him, but another time I simply asked for a check, and he gave me one for $5k. This was all amazingly new and wonderful to me.

Let's see…waitressing for $2.00 an hour plus flirting and begging for tips…or a Sugar Daddy who hands over $17K without breaking a sweat in the first six months? Hmm…I can't decide…which shall it be?

Anyone that doesn't respect these choices, or at least adopt a "live and let live" attitude is, in my opinion, being a narrow-minded prig (and probably clueless about the ways of the world). The Sugar life is not without its challenges, but it's a lot more enjoyable and a lot less exhausting than most traditional paths.

And yet, if there's one single aspect of the Sugar lifestyle that sets tongues wagging among the conventional, it's the money; money in exchange for sex. In online commentaries and message boards, Sugar Daddies are frequently referred to as pimps, while Sugar Babies get labeled prostitutes. Never mind that a pimp is someone who sells a woman's services to other men and pockets most of the profits, which isn't even remotely what Sugar Daddyhood is about. Apparently most people aren't bright enough to see the distinction, or else they don't know what a Sugar Daddy is, just that it involves sex and money and therefore must be wicked.

If only they knew the half of it, they'd probably be even more outraged! The fact is, money has a significance that goes far beyond the practical, in the Sugar lifestyle as elsewhere. Money carries a weight of meaning, symbolism, and associations. Some of these meanings are universal, others as individual as thumb prints. Some of money's associations are erotic. Says one Sugar Baby:

> After much thought to get at the root of my wants and desires, I've realized that, emotionally, I want to be someone's expensive dirty little secret. To me there's something incredibly erotic about an illicit affair that centers upon me being a toy, allowed to go out only when Sugar Daddy wants to play without the complications of everyday life, with no strings, no attachments. Well, that, my friend, has its price. Many girls allow themselves to be treated this way in relationships —

essentially giving it away. Not this SB.

—*from the SeekingArrangement.com blog*

And that, my friend, is one pretty sharp – and honest – Sugar Babe!

It's Not All About The Money...

"I was with this guy, getting physical, and he said he wanted me to go downtown. I said, downtown, huh...so, I started kissing my way down his chest and stomach, and when I got downtown, I just looked. I was lookin' and examining like maybe there was something I was interested in. He said: *what you doin?* I said: *I'm looking, that's whatcha do when you get sent downtown without no money, you look.*"

—*A comedy routine on* Comicview

That's the kind of humor you'll find on the SeekingArrangement blog, where three-quarters of the chatters are Babies rather than Dads. They make jokes about it, and complain about cheapskates, but most Sugar Babies aren't in it strictly for the money, believe it or not – and if you don't believe it yet, you will after you've read this chapter.

Money has never been the motivating factor. I originally got on this site looking for excitement. I could have a boyfriend if I wanted, but I find them to be annoying and more trouble than they're worth at this point in my life! Eventually I will, of course, want to seriously date someone, but I'm 21 and right now that's not on the agenda!

· · · · ·

I definitely did not get into this to make ends meet! I wanted the excitement, the special treatment from someone I can be myself with. The extra cash is nice, but I would never get into an arrangement if I didn't feel really good about my SD. I consider this dating with benefits!

· · · · ·

It really isn't the allowance I get excited about, it's the extra things like presents and pre-paid spa visits, and shopping...things I would never spend my own money on. That's what gets me the most excited about having a Sugar Daddy.

Those are just the tip of the iceberg. Sure, most Sugar Babies admit that the money's nice – but it's not their only motivating factor.

The funny thing is, when a guy complains about spending his money on her, or makes her feel bad for expressing her financial needs, *then* it becomes a huge issue for a Sugar Baby. A cheap Sugar Daddy tends to make Sugar Babies mad, and rightfully so: she's following the rules of Sugar dating; he should too. What's more, it's humiliating to be told you're not worth that much money, or you should pay half the bill, or you spent too much on something. A man who wants to be a Sugar Daddy has to learn to be gracious about it, to give without resentment or grudge.

Nothing turns a woman off as much as a cheapskate. I know one woman who stuck it out with her wealthy but cheap husband for over 20 years, until their kid was grown, and then gave him his walking papers. He'd been so tight-fisted about things like fixing up the house, things he'd benefit from just as much as her, that she couldn't wait to squeeze as much as possible out of him in the divorce. If women feel that way about men in traditional relationships, how do you think they feel about a cheap Sugar Daddy? This is a guy who, by registering on a Sugar website, tacitly promises to be generous. Then he turns around and breaks the agreement – or he keeps it, but with bad vibes. Hell hath no fury like a Sugar Baby Promised Sugar but Given Splenda!

One confirmed Sugar Daddy says, only half facetiously:

> Having a Sugar Baby is a lot like being married, except you pay ahead of time. In marriage you pay after the divorce. Why not just pay up front?

Celebrities like Madonna and Paul McCartney are perfect examples of how married breadwinners end up paying a much higher price than Sugar Daddies and Sugar Mommas when it's all said and done. Madonna's 10 year marriage to Guy Richie ended up costing her over $76 million. If she had kept Guy as a sugar baby with a $20,000 monthly allowance, not only would she have more fun along the way, her total cost would have been a comparatively thrifty $2.4 million for those 10 years. Paul McCartney's dump of gold digger ex-wife of 7 years, Heather Mills, cost him $48.6 million. Had he chosen to keep her as a sugar baby with a $20,000 a month allowance instead, he would have only spent $1.68 million.

···But Then Again, Sometimes It's All Money, All The Time

In my dreams I have a plan
If I got me a wealthy man
I wouldn't have to work at all
I'd fool around and have a ball.
Money, money, money
must be funny
in the rich man's world.

—*Money, Money, Money.* ABBA

I'm astounded every time I hear about an alleged Sugar Daddy like the one in this Sugar Baby's post:

We met at a fantastic restaurant just after the lunch crowd was leaving, so there were very few people there. We had a great time talking, were comfortable with each other, and he seemed to be very much into me. Great ambiance, great food, although I had those butterflies and couldn't eat very much, a great martini and most of all great conversation.

Then the check came. He pushed it towards me and said, "I got it last time. Your turn." I don't know what his reasoning was and I really don't care. I was speechless but somehow kept my composure. I politely told him that I wasn't sure what his understanding was of our arrangement, but there was no doubt in my mind as to my understanding, and it did not include picking up the check. He sat back in his seat and thoughtfully said: Well, for an $85 lunch, you'd better be a great ----. I excused myself from the table and walked out, got into my car and left.

This is a typical example of the clueless Daddy, and the picture she paints is so vivid I don't need to cite any more horror stories; taken all together, they can be harrowing. I suspect that a guy who pulls something like this hasn't read a single word on the website, never tasted Sugar in his life, and has no idea what it's about. He's probably using SeekingArrangement.com as if it were just a regular online dating service, paying no attention to what people here are trying to accomplish. That, Daddies, is a great big boo-boo. (He is also, in my opinion, lacking in everyday notions of politesse.)

In the interests of minimizing misunderstandings of this nature, I suggest every man reading this who's either registered or thinking about registering as a Sugar Daddy go onto the site and read every single word available to be read. If you've already written your profile, go back to it now, and if you haven't, listen up before you do.

There's a line item in the profile that says: *My Budget*. This does *not* mean, "My monthly household expenses and income." It does *not* mean, "How much money I plan to earn and spend this year." It does *not* mean, "Wishful thinking." It means this: ***The exact amount of disposable income I have each month, after paying my expenses, which I am able and <u>willing</u> to spend on a Sugar Baby.*** Understand? This is very important! If you do not have disposable income and you are unable to spend anything on a Sugar Baby – or, just as important, ***unwilling*** – then close the profile without saving it, and make your way over to e-harmony or match.com to look for a girlfriend. This site is not meant for finding girlfriends. ***It is for Sugar Daddies and Sugar Babies.***

If you've passed that hurdle and decided that yes, you have disposable income and yes, you're able ***and willing*** to spend it on a Sugar Baby, then welcome. When you browse through the Sugar Baby profiles, notice that they have a category corresponding to "My Budget." Theirs says "What I Expect." This is where they say how much money they would like to receive each month, from a Sugar Daddy, in an arrangement.

Now do what you do when calculating your taxes: Write down on a piece of paper the amount of your budget. Underneath that figure, write down the amount of money the Sugar Baby says she expects. If the second number is larger than the first, click on your mouse and move on. If it is smaller, subtract it from the larger number. That's the disposable income you have after paying a Sugar Baby, either to be added to Sugar Baby's fund, or used for something else. It is inadvisable to contact those Sugar Babies whose financial expectations exceed your budget!

Sugar Babies: You bear some responsibility for avoiding

misunderstandings. Your job is to be clear and honest about what you expect in the money department. If you know the amount of money you want from a Sugar Daddy, don't low-ball the figure, but bravely write it down. Even if it seems high, that's all right: you'll attract those men who can afford it and want to give it to you. Remember, a lot of Sugar Daddies genuinely *want* to give you a decent monthly allowance, and the profile is the last place for you to be shy. You can always change the figure later, but this is the position from which you should begin negotiating. Here's what one Sugar Daddy has to say about Sugar Babies' financial IQs:

> I am surprised at how little most SBs understand their finances. In most situations, I find that she isn't asking for enough to meet her needs, especially when it comes to paying back credit cards or other debt. She needs to consider the time and cost it takes to get ready for her SD… getting dolled up, shopping for extras (food, lingerie, wine), picking up the babysitter. Most are surprised when I offer more. I may be overly generous, but my philosophy is a happy SB makes for a happy SD.

As pointed out, not every Sugar Baby expects, or even wants, a cash allowance, but she does want gifts, trips to the spa, fine meals in restaurants, travel, expenses paid, etc. In that case you should enter "Open – Negotiable." In my opinion that's the only time you should enter "Negotiable," in the money spaces; leaving one of the most important items in your profile a mystery makes misunderstandings more likely. Money is a loaded issue, after all. The more matter-of-fact, up front and honest you are about it now, the easier it will be to deal with later on. Also, many people do not respond to profiles that aren't specific.

Bear in mind that whatever you put into a profile, it is not sealed in cement. Someone once told me that every unsigned contract is merely a negotiating tool. The same could be said for your profile: its purpose is to attract the kind of people who are right for you, weed out inappropriate candidates, and serve as a blueprint for negotiations.

We've covered clueless, cheap or unwilling Sugar Daddies; now it's time to talk about another part of the story – greedy little Sugar Babies who manipulate and wheedle and whine and scam. Sugar Baby scams are covered elsewhere in this book; but some Sugar Babies aren't exactly "scamming," they're just grabby and obnoxious:

> I had a woman recently email me and say, "As a SD you are supposed to pay my rent and I'll be your SB on the side...and don't ask me any other questions." This was after I just basically said hello – but maybe she thinks this is how things work.

Who raises the money topic first? When? Should it be discussed during the email phase? (Probably not.) On the first date? How will the money be transferred? By check? Cash? On a regular monthly schedule? On a per diem or per date basis, or as a monthly allowance? Should a Sugar Baby get a gift on the first date?

Will they have sex the first time they meet? Should he or she raise the subject? Should they work out a schedule of regular visits? Will they have sex every time? What if there's no chemistry? What if one isn't attracted to the other? How do you tell someone you aren't attracted to them? Or that you don't want to go any further, for whatever reason?

These questions get raised on the blog all the time; typically,

Sugar Babies ask about money, Daddies ask about sex. Women have a hard time bringing up money, understandably so. The kindest thing a Sugar Daddy can do on or even before a first date is to bring it up himself, in a matter-of-fact way, thus sparing her the agony.

> I've been talking to a total sweetie for months now through IM and emails, and he finally asked to meet me. He's coming to my city, since he is a gentleman, for dinner. The other day we discussed logistics (my allowance and number of visits and things like that). We had never talked about an allowance before, and he was the one who brought it up, which I was glad about. I'd been so happy getting to know him I had actually forgotten that we hadn't discussed it.

Here's a radical idea: just as it would be a kindness for Sugar Daddy to initiate the money conversation, *what if Sugar Baby was the one to start talking sex?* Can you even imagine it? How about it, Babies? Give it a try. While you're sitting there talking about your lives or movies or whatever, find an opening where you can steer the talk onto the subject of sex, and say something like, *What's your idea of how sex fits into this arrangement?* I have a hunch Daddy will be floored – and he'll probably think you're the greatest gal on the face of the earth. *Caveat:* Some men are turned off by sexual assertiveness in a woman. If he is…do you really want him?

One Sugar Baby said she was sick of playing mind games, and she wrote, facetiously, what she'd like to say to a potential Sugar Daddy on a first meeting:

> Hi, yeah you're gorgeous, too…hmm so, what are you thinking in terms of an allowance or one time large gifts? Uh huh, so the first is good for me…what are you looking for? Yeah, yeah- write it down on this paper so I can make sure I cross everything off of the list. Oh, okay, you

like six-inch heels? I need money for "props" up front, papa. Yeah, AmEx is fine- call and put me on as a user... okay. So, are we gonna fuck or what?...

Come on, now, admit it: that would be refreshing, wouldn't it?

Attitudes about the money and sex aspects of Sugar relationships are all over the place; nobody has just the "right" approach or solution. Some typical male comments:

> It is very difficult to find a balance where you can get to know someone without the guy feeling pressured to shell out thousands right away, and without the girl feeling pressured for sex.
>
> • • • • •
>
> In my opinion, once the SB says she wants money to meet, that leaves the door open for me to convey what I want in return for my money. Is that wrong?
>
> • • • • •
>
> What I'd prefer is to take care of travel expenses and see if we click. Then, if things progressed, I'd be more than happy to help financially at the end of the weekend. I really dislike the whole "pay for play" deal, but if she says she needs cash, from now on I'm going to say what I need.

Some Sugar Daddies give cash or another gift on a first meeting, primarily to prove they're serious.

> What I have done on a few previous dates and with an SB I had for a short time is to take her hand under the table and gently put $$ in it – $100–$200 – and say that this a donation to the "Jenny financial independence fund" or something silly like that. It makes the point that I want to help and it's NSA – but sets the expectation that I am serious. My thought is that the amount increases with each date until we get to a set agreement.

In an earlier chapter we talked about preparing mentally for Sugar dating, and one suggestion for Sugar Daddies was to examine their attitudes around spending, or giving away, money. The same self-scrutiny applies to Sugar Babies, and to both genders' attitudes about giving and receiving, not only money but tangible gifts and intangible kindnesses.

Giving and Receiving

I'm not worried about the economy - I put all my money into high maintenance women.
—Dave Letterman

Most people understand that gift-giving is an art requiring a certain degree of thought and knowledge of the recipient's taste, likes and dislikes. But receiving is also an art, perhaps even more difficult. Since a big part of a Sugar relationship is about giving and receiving – tangible as well as intangible gifts – it's a good idea to look at your attitudes in this area.

Some Sugar Babies tend to be overly grateful for Sugar Daddy's beneficence. If a girl isn't used to being with guys who have the wherewithal and desire to buy her gifts and take her to pricey restaurants, she'll have to learn to accept Sugar Daddy's generosity with charm and grace. She should never say, "Oh, you shouldn't have," or "You're too good to me," or, worst of all, "I don't deserve this."

Listen up, Sugar Babes: *You do deserve it*! That's what a Sugar Baby is *for*—to be adored and pampered and coddled and given to. Phony self-deprecation can come off as a lack of gratitude, and that's a real turn-off to a generous Daddy. Besides, when a Sugar Baby doesn't have to worry about money and struggle to pay the bills, her time and attention are freed up for her Daddy – which is the whole point! I'm not saying Sugar Babies sit home preening and making themselves beautiful for their Daddies all day long; hopefully they're pursuing their own goals, whether that's school or art or auditions or starting a business. But the Sugar Baby part of her life is work, even if she enjoys it; who says you have to hate your job? She *should* be well-paid.

Ironically, some savvy Daddies are more cognizant of this than Babies. The classic classy Sugar Daddy showers his Sugar Baby with gifts and pays for necessities not because he *has* to, but because he *wants* to. Making her life easier and more pleasant gives him a feeling of accomplishment. He *likes* being magnanimous, or else he wouldn't be doing the Sugar thing in the first place. Taking care of a Sugar Baby brings him joy – but if she keeps insisting she doesn't deserve it, he might just start to believe her!

One Sugar Baby was reluctant to suggest expensive activities. She suffered from an overriding sense that, since he paid for everything, only he had the right to choose how they spent time and money. Once, when they were in the Caribbean, she was dying to rent a yacht and go island hopping, but he nixed the idea. In the face of his resistance she backed off, thinking "well, after all, it *is* his money."

When they got home, he told her he regretted not having done what she wanted. He said her ideas always turned out to be great fun, and his resistance was just a curmudgeonly habit left over from his marriage to a mercenary wife. Not only did he make it up to her by taking her island hopping – he went out and *bought a yacht!*

Sugar Babies – and Daddies too! – should learn to *value everything they give one another as much as they value his money*. Admittedly, this is not a terribly easy thing to do. We live in a world, and particularly in a country, that functions under an economic system in which money is prized out of all proportion to what it should be relative to other parts of life.

Ten dollars is ten dollars is ten dollars – but an idea has no price. The gift of making someone laugh carries no dollar amount. Because clear-cut monetary values of money are so deeply ingrained in us, we have no idea *how* to gauge the value of intangibles. Even if Sugar Baby cooks Sugar Daddy an elegant meal, we'd hardly know how to place a value on it other than to add up the cost of the ingredients. Cooking a meal for someone is an act of love – and we already know what our society thinks about exchanging love for money! Sugar Baby's intangible gifts, under our cultural mindset, carry no value. Of course, we know this isn't true (Just ask Sugar Daddy how much he values her back rubs). We simply do not have any system of measurement for these kinds of things, and that lack translates into a difficulty showing our appreciation for acts of love and kindness.

But in a Sugar relationship it's important to show appreciation for everything, including, but not limited to, spending money. Remember, practice makes perfect – so practice at every opportunity, with your Sugar and with anyone else who gives you something or does something nice for you. Practice saying a genuine "Thank you." Don't be embarrassed to say it; if you are, keep saying it until it loses its charge. Learn not to minimize appreciation.

Learn also how to *receive* appreciation. Don't dismiss whatever you're being thanked for by saying or acting like it was no big deal. You can actually ruin someone's joy by minimizing the gift you gave them.

Learn to say you want something when you do. If Sugar Daddy asks if you want something, and you do but you say you don't, you're committing Sugar crime. This is about getting what you want, remember? It's about being honest and up front. It's not about self-denial and self-sacrifice: *Yecch!* Those words give me the creeps! People are always acting like self-sacrifice is such a high ideal, or proof of love. Why? Why do I have to sacrifice myself to prove or express love for someone else? Why should I, or anyone? Self-sacrifice is another one of those cultural myths.

The truth is that, even though some Sugar Babies aren't as dazzled as others by dollar signs, Sugar dating and money are inextricably connected. Said one Sugar Baby, "He makes so much money, and just a little can make such a huge difference in my life."

While money is certainly important for the sugar daddy, what he spends on his Sugar Baby is, by most accounts, entertainment money. For the Sugar Baby, it is often so much more; sure, for a few high-living gals it may mean an expensive designer dress or the plastic surgery they've always dreamed of – but for most Sugar Babies it represents the rent, the late electric bill, tuition, or the answer to a less stressful life. As such, money has *everything* to do with sugar relationships. It's the glue that binds them.

CHAPTER 5:

DIPPING INTO THE SUGAR BOWL

Once you decide this lifestyle is for you, a little prep work is in order before you delve into the Sugar Bowl. Both Babies and Daddies should spend some time doing mental and emotional work even before searching for one another. Remember, this is a *mutually beneficial relationship*. That means that each side must have something to offer the other. Only you know what your something is. If you're not sure now, by the end of this chapter you will be, as I'm going to lead you through a fierce – and fun – self-inventory.

Your search for a Sugar Daddy calls for a whole new way of looking at yourself. You have to stare down your assets and flaws with a coolly critical eye, adopting a practical and pragmatic point of view. Actually, you don't *have* to – but if you're really serious about achieving your goals, then the way you go about obtaining them should be equally serious.

In your quest for a Sugar Daddy, you're going to be competing with hundreds of others, and to stand a good chance, you'd better know what makes you special compared to the next aspiring Sugar Baby. You need to be on familiar terms with your specific attributes, and know what to emphasize and what to downplay. You need to determine if there's anything you want or have to change about yourself.

As you conduct your self-inventory, try to maintain a sense of humor and a degree of emotional detachment. This process is a lot easier when emotions are left out of it. That doesn't mean you should be cynical, though. Think logic. Think reality.

Youth, beauty and intelligence are valuable assets. It might seem cold to think in those terms, but it just happens to be the way things are. Even in the conventional dating scene, people are constantly evaluating one another. Some of it may be subconscious, but it's happening just the same. They're categorizing positive traits as assets and negative ones as drawbacks, and basing their dating choices on these assessments. Remember too, that one person's negative might be another one's positive, so don't make quick assumptions. For instance, one woman might love to hear jokes, so if a man told them all the time she'd put that personality trait into the positive category, while a woman who hates jokes would classify it as negative. Another example: many people consider self-introspection depressing, or "negative," while some people enjoy it immensely and would list a leaning towards it as positive.

When you register on SeekingArrangement.com, you'll be writing up a profile of yourself. (We'll go into this in greater detail in Chapter Five.) This profile is the first impression potential Sugar Daddies will get of you. People on the blog say they don't bother responding to general profiles that don't give enough information about the person, so the more specific you are, the better. As you work on your self-inventory, keep this profile in the back of your mind.

The two primary categories of questions you should be able to answer with ease and confidence are (1) What do you have to offer? and (2) What do you want in exchange? Let's start with the first.

Caveat: This is a process of inner exploration, of getting to know yourself. While it can be a lifelong endeavor, taking a look at who you are at this moment in time will do for our purposes. Still, you're most likely not going to zip through this in a few minutes; it's going to take some time.

Sit down with a pen, paper and respond to the following statements and questions. For the statements, write down whether you agree with them, and why. For the questions, write down your answers. There are no right or wrong answers, and no scoring. This isn't a test you can pass or fail, but a tool to help you with your self-inventory.

- My motto is *Live and Let Live*.
- I pride myself on being different.
- Do you present yourself in ways that differ from who you are?

- Do you keep your promises?
- I am easy to get to know.
- I am an outgoing person.
- It's easy for me to be affectionate with a lover.
- I want my partner to understand me deeply.
- Do you worry about being abandoned by your lover?
- Do you find it easy to get close to romantic partners?
- How do you like your partners to show affection? Gifts? Hugs? Kisses? Or?
- Do you need constant reassurance and affection from partners?
- Do you frequently act on your first impulses, or do you squelch them?
- When you don't get what you want are you unhappy? Angry?
- Do you persist until you get what you want, or do you give up easily?
- It's my way or the highway.
- I'm uncomfortable with strong emotion.
- I can calm myself down when I'm under stress.
- When I get angry, I have good/poor self-control
- Do you worry? What are the things you worry about?
- I like to attend gatherings where I can meet new people.
- I enjoy exploring new places.
- I have a broad range of interests and activities.
- Large social gatherings exhaust/exhilarate me.
- Where do you see yourself five years from now?

When you finish, leave the list and go out for a walk, to a movie, anywhere...just get your mind off it for a short while. Later, or the next day, return and, being brutally honest, change anything that doesn't ring absolutely true.

Now that you've conducted your fearless self-inventory, it's time to pinpoint exactly what you think you can offer a Sugar Daddy. Make a list of attributes you possess that are likely to bring pleasure to another person, for example, "beautiful," or "spontaneous" or "great cook." Don't be shy or self-deprecating! Think about what other people have said about you – maybe you're known for having a great sense of humor, or for always being there for your friends. Take your time with this; you might want to add to or refine it over time as more of your assets occur to you. Save this list to use later on in your profile.

Now for the second category: What do you want in exchange? Some of this might also go into your profile, but more importantly, these are questions you should be prepared to ask potential Sugar Daddies.

- How often do you want to meet?
- Would you prefer your SD to be married or single?
- Are you willing to include sex in the relationship? If so, how often?
- Do you want to be monogamous, or do you want other lovers?
- Do you want to travel? On short trips, or longer ones?
- Do you want your SD to pay some or all of your bills / rent?
- Do you want an allowance? How much? A credit card?
- Do you want help with: financial planning / your career / college tuition / a new business?
- Are there anything else you want from your SD? Networking opportunities perhaps? Career mentoring?

Do the same thing you did with the first category of questions – leave it for awhile, then come back and make any necessary changes or revisions.

One difference between conventional and Sugar dating is that the former can be anything from a pleasant way to spend an evening or a step in the hunt for a spouse. Sugar dating is different than this. To put it into blunt language: Sugar dating is *barter.*

You should consider the fact – and I do mean the cold hard, *fact* – that in negotiating a Sugar relationship, you're using the gift of your youth and beauty for material gain. How do you feel about that? Can you take a coolly logical view of it as just the way things are? Or even better, a smart move on your part? To carry on a relationship of this kind requires a certain detachment. You don't want to end up feeling badly about yourself. Conversely, you don't want to get carried away by your own desirability, becoming arrogant and conceited if your looks fetch the finest grade of Sugar on the market.

Spend some time thinking about the kind of Sugar Baby you want to be. Do you see yourself as a friendly companion, rewarded for your time with a higher standard of living? Or as a "kept" mistress, with all your financial needs taken care of and most of your time and energy devoted to Sugar Daddy's happiness? Or do you want to be somewhere between those two extremes?

If you aren't sure, I suggest you do some visualization exercises. The following exercise works for any kind of soul-searching or decision-making. If you already practice meditation or creative visualization or any similar kind of tool, then use that method. If not, here are some simplified instructions:

Sit on the floor, legs crossed Buddha-style, or in a chair, legs on the floor, whichever way you're most comfortable. Close your eyes. Let your breath flow naturally. Take your time. Envision a quiet, relaxing place in nature – a beach, or forest, or a sunny meadow; whatever relaxes you. Notice your breathing. Don't change your breath, just watch it, and if it changes, notice that too. Do this for five or ten minutes, or until you're totally at peace.

Now replace the nature scene in your mind's eye with an image of yourself as a Sugar Baby. What sort of picture pops into your head? Are you with your Sugar Daddy? Or are you alone waiting for him? Whether with him or not, what are you doing? What are you wearing? How do you feel? Are you happy? Contented? Frightened? Excited? If you don't like the scene, change it. Refine the picture until you settle on one you like.

Practice this exercise once a day during your Sugar search, refining your inner visions until you can fully imagine your ideal situation. If you do this, then by the time you talk to a Sugar Daddy you should know exactly what you want from an arrangement.

And then you'll meet someone who fulfills none of these requirements, get hit by a jolt of electricity, and run off with him forever! Just kidding! That's exactly what we're trying to avoid by entering into arranged relationships in the first place.

I was only half joking, though: as they say, "the best laid plans" are often turned upside down by something unforeseen. You can predict and calculate and plan all you want, and then someone or something unpredictable comes along to upset the apple cart. Still, when you set out on your Sugar search knowing who you are and what you want, you're starting from a better place.

STOP!

Just when it seems the time has come to take that sweet sugar dip…you'd better duck, because here comes another monkey wrench.

It shouldn't surprise any woman to hear this, but it might not have occurred to some of you: when it comes to self-presentation, *men lie!*

That's right! A few guys misrepresent themselves on SeekingArrangement and similar websites, putting on an elaborate charade of wealth and power, when in reality they have none.

> This so-called SD made sure I stopped talking to everyone on the site by telling me to close my profile. He claimed he was a billionaire and promised me a credit card and allowance. We were supposed to meet at a high-class hotel, but when I got there he claimed he'd lost his wallet…I did a background check on him. He made $20,000 a year.
>
> • • • • •
>
> One Sugar Daddy assured me he'd set me up in a plush resort with a minimum of $3000 spending money for the week. After arriving in LA I found out I'd be lodging in a motel, and he gave me $500, most of which I spent on cab fare and meals. On the day he knew I was leaving, he didn't answer his phone, and I had to take a cab to the airport and buy my own plane ticket home.
>
> • • • • •
>
> He will tell you that he'll put you up in a five-star hotel, and fly you in from anywhere, and that a plane ticket home is available if you don't click. If you decide not to have sex with him, he will promptly drop you off at the airport with a fake flight confirmation number.

Some men don't actually lie, but are clueless as to what this Sugar Daddy business is all about – they're just using the site as a way to meet beautiful women for conventional dating.

So how do you distinguish the Sugar from the Splenda?

It's not impossible to spot a fake Daddy, but to do so you've got to be thinking and seeing clearly. Remember that cool detachment I mentioned? You can't afford to get swept off your feet on a first date, or to let wishful fantasies prevent you from seeing the reality right in front of you. This is not to imply that you must conduct your search under a perpetual cloud of suspicion – but at the very least you should maintain a healthy dose of disbelief early on.

A few signs to watch out for:

- In his email correspondence, does his grammar and spelling imply an educational or job level other than what he's indicated? Unfortunately, typos and grammatical errors are common in email, but you should be able to tell if someone's just being fast and casual, or if he's seriously deficient (cutting him some slack if English is his second language).

- Does he contradict himself? I once sat next to a man in a hotel lobby loudly talking on his cell phone; he named a different city as his home to the three successive woman he spoke to.

- It's probably inadvisable to have more than one drink on a first date with a Sugar Daddy, since alcohol clouds clarity and dulls your senses (even though it sometimes feels the opposite).

- Most unmarried Sugar Daddies will give you their real name. If so, always do a Google search to verify their job.

- You can do a background search on anyone online for a fee. Search public records by name, run a reverse phone number search, look him up on a reverse address directory.

- On first meetings, before you decide to enter an arrangement, ask to see their driver's license to verify age and home address.
- Many men give fake profiles to protect their identity.
- Some Sugar Babies prepare a few questions that only someone who travels in wealthy sophisticated circles could answer, about high fashion, finance, culture, or cuisine. Don't drill the guy, but find a way to casually work these kinds of questions, or allusions to places or people, into the conversation. (Just be sure you don't sound as if you're name-dropping or he'll think *you're* the phony!)
- Once you've registered on SeekingArrangement.com, you'll be able to visit and read the blog. This is probably the best place to find ways of dealing with fake Sugar Daddies. It's also where Sugar Babies unload horror stories like the ones previously mentioned, and post warnings about specific Fake Daddies.
- You can tell a few things about a person by the place they choose to meet, the way they dress, the way they talk, and the kind of car they drive – *but not always*. Some Sugar Daddies dress in Topsiders, T-Shirt and Khakis…just before climbing back onto their yachts. On the other hand, anyone can rent a Ferrari for a day, buy a fake Rolex in Chinatown, and wear Armani marked down several times at Nordstrom Rack.

Assessing wealth takes a certain kind of radar. You either have that skill or you don't – or you try to develop it. One experienced Sugar Baby offers this laundry list of cues to a man's wealth (or lack thereof):

ugly shoes, old socks, bad nails, bad teeth (not natural defects but bad hygiene and things that any rich man could have and should have had fixed) bad haircuts, a cheap cell phone and he talks about how many minutes he can use without going over, buying cheap seats at the ballgame because "they are really the best" when anyone knows they aren't, He might want to keep his personal life private, especially if he's married, but there should be signs of his profession – business calls, knowledge of various topics, enough to let you know he isn't sweeping floors at Wal-Mart. If he takes you shopping and steers you toward clearance.

I hope I'm not giving the impression that there aren't real Daddies out there. There most definitely are.

I look at the SB/SD relationship much as a man and his mistress – a complex relationship with multiple levels, emotional, sexual and maybe even spiritual. Just as you support a wife in many cases, you support a mistress, even though women these days have many options.

• • • • •

SBs get financial support, mentoring, friendship and somebody who truly does care about them and may even love them. (I have an easy time loving women – they are wonderful.) They also get stability, and sex – and hopefully a mature SD knows what he's doing more so than younger men.

This guy is obviously the real thing.

SeekingArrangement maintains an upper-level membership, the Diamond Club, for Certified Sugar Daddies, whose identity, income, and net worth have all been verified. Because their credentials have been proven, Sugar Babies know right off the bat that Diamond Club Members mean business.

It's important to recognize that finding the right situation might take a long time – months, even years. If you expect to hit a home run your first at- bat, you're going to be disappointed. You have to go into this with your eyes wide open, prepared for setbacks. Anything worth having is worth waiting for, so don't get discouraged if you get a lot of rhinestones on your way to the Harry Winston's. You just need to be aware of the fakes, and learn to protect yourself from them.

Caution: Rough Road Ahead

A savvy Sugar Baby should take other kinds of precautions as well. Online dating, like using classified ads, going on blind dates and similar ways of meeting people always carries a risk; it goes with the territory. If you've never done this kind of dating – or even if you have – you might not know the rules of the game.

- Always meet for the first time – maybe even the first few times – in a public place like a café or restaurant. Bars aren't recommended, for the simple reason that you want to keep alcohol consumption to a minimum. Also, some bars or lounges are too noisy for conversation – you don't want to miss half of what SD has to say.

- Whenever possible, verify details. You can't put an insurance policy on an arrangement, but you can take steps to verify promises that are made. For instance, if staying at a hotel is part of your arrangement, verify the booking yourself.

- Never go anywhere without enough money for an emergency (this used to be called "Mad Money") and a plan for getting yourself home, if necessary.

- Let a friend know where you're going and when you expect to be home, and have someone call you at random during your date.

- Don't give out your address until you trust someone. You probably shouldn't tell him where you work either, or give out other geographical information. This isn't because all men are axe murderers until proven otherwise; it's because some men have poor social skills, and may try to hang on even after being rejected, hanging around outside a woman's door or office. This sort of thing is more annoying than dangerous, but you certainly want to avoid it.

- Always practice safe sex unless and until your arrangement becomes monogamous, at which point you might both agree to be tested for HIV and other STDs before abandoning precautions. Sometimes wealthy, powerful men feel invincible and think they can't possibly catch anything. Unfortunately, a virus doesn't distinguish between rich and poor.

- Don't accept personal checks from someone you do not know well. If the SD turns out to be a fake, he may cancel payment on the check and you may be stuck with a huge bill from your bank. If this happens, even after you've been warned not to accept a personal check, you should seek advice from a lawyer and consider filing a lawsuit. If the check is forged, that's a felony, contact law enforcement immediately!

Straight from the horse's mouth: Following are some precautions posted on the blog from those who know, Sugar Babes themselves:

> If the information he's asking for is of a sexual nature, I would avoid him as he might be a pervert; a true SD shows a little class, and he's looking for more than a quickie.

· · · · ·

Never go to the house of someone you don't know. Always meet in a public place like a coffee shop or a mall where there are plenty of people around and you can park without him seeing where your car is. A gentleman will come to you: after all a Sugar Daddy is supposed to be successful and have money, so driving to see you should be no problem for him. A lady should always be on her home turf in familiar surroundings. Let a friend know what you are doing. Never take off to some strange town you don't know. Once you get to know him and if he's trustworthy, then you can travel to see him, or better yet have him send you a plane ticket.

• • • • •

(1) When traveling, I prefer to bring a girlfriend with me. If he can afford 10–20k a month allowance, surely he can afford to pay for my friend. (2) I do not want a SD picking me up at the airport; please send a car for me. (3) Meet me in the hotel bar, not in my room. (4) Where can I Google you?

• • • • •

Whenever I meet a guy I text a close friend and give her the guy's info. If she doesn't hear from me in a certain time frame she's to take action. I always call when I land, or am on the phone just when I'm meeting the guy so he knows about her.

Grooming Yourself for Sugar Dating

At last we arrive at the purely fun part of this chapter, the area of preparation that every girly-girl loves: grooming yourself for a dip in the Sugar Bowl.

In the Julia Roberts movie, *Pretty Woman*, no one took her character seriously until she started to dress and act like someone who could conceivably be a companion to Richard Gere's successful businessman character. Even before he took her into the hotel he threw his coat over her tacky Hollywood Boulevard Hooker attire. All of which is a way of stating the obvious: if you want to attract a rich, successful man, you have to look the part.

For a Sugar Baby, looks and image are of utmost importance. If a Sugar Daddy has the choice between an average-looking woman or a knockout, we all know which one he'll choose. The good news is that every average-looking woman can transform herself into a knockout.

The female of the species has so many options when it comes to style of dress, makeup, hair, and accessories, that the same woman can look entirely different each night of the week (just be careful not to go bald from hair product overuse!). It's your call as to how much of a transformation you make. The range of possibilities is wide – as simple as a new hair style or as radical as cosmetic surgery.

You might want to take another self-inventory, this time of your appearance. Begin at the top, with your hair, assessing the color, style, length, degree of curl, etc. Decide what changes your hair might need, if any, and then proceed to the hair salon without passing Go. Unless you're an experienced stylist yourself, this is no time for do-it-yourself hair. Besides, when you're a Sugar Baby you'll be making weekly salon visits, so start getting used to it.

Since most women know how to make themselves look terrific, I'm not going to run through the entire beauty regimen except to provide a checklist of points to focus on:

☐ Hair

☐ Skin (face, neck, elbows, feet)
☐ Makeup
☐ Nails (fingers and toes)
☐ Hands
☐ Body Hair (eyebrows, legs, underarms, pubes)

Now comes the big decision: *What to Wear*. For a first meeting in a café or restaurant, unless it's five-star dining, you'll want to look a precise degree of casual. As most women know, the trick is to look simultaneously fabulous and as if it took you five minutes to get ready. This is achieved primarily by understatement. You might have spent forty-five minutes on your makeup, yet it's barely visible to the untrained eye (and most men's eyes are pretty untrained when it comes to makeup). Even if you obsessed for three days, trying on everything in your closet, you should look as if you just stepped into whatever happened to catch your eye. The idea you want to convey is that you're so gorgeous you look it, no matter what you wrap your body in.

While most Sugar Daddies don't expect you to be wearing designer clothing, they do want to see a touch of class. On the SeekingArrangement blog, one Daddy complained that a Sugar Baby wore a dress she obviously bought at Wal-Mart. Prior to their meeting she hinted at a fairly large allowance requirement, so the cheap clothes were a major turn-off.

Wearing cheap clothing isn't the same as looking like you just threw something on – if the latter is of good quality, it says that *everything* in your closet is. Cheap clothing, on the other hand, speaks of a mediocre life and a mind devoid of imagination. It tells a potential SD that not only haven't you earned much money, but you haven't managed to snag a generous benefactor – so why should *he* be the first sap? Either that, or you're clueless – you don't know the difference between quality and trash, you don't realize that he does, and therefore you're not sophisticated enough to make it as a high-class Sugar Baby.

Classy second-hand clothing is preferable to cheap polyester rags from Wal-Mart. If you're not comfortable shopping for and wearing previously worn clothes, you can still go upscale for less at discount outlets, or watch for major sales at Nordstrom or Bloomingdales. If all else fails, raid your girlfriends' closets. (What are friends for?)

> I bring a gift to a first meeting to show I am serious. I am meeting her to determine if she is also serious, and if she's someone with SB potential for me. I want to see how she carries on a conversation, if she has a good personality, how she acts in public, if she's polished, and of course her appearance. I want to know if this is some-one I can be with and take out with confidence. If she prepares herself to show she is polished and that she knows how to act with a successful man such as myself, that shows me she is serious.

If you wear jewelry, make it understated and genuine, i.e., don't pile on the beads and bangles from The Dollar Store. That's fine for clubbing with your girlfriends, but for a date with a potential Sugar Daddy you're better off with the simple lapis pendant your parents gave you for graduation. All men love women who look good in a little black dress.

Talking About Talking

On a first date, or even on subsequent meetings, you might nervously wonder what you and Sugar Daddy will find to talk about.

While you want to be warm and personable, you don't want to blurt out your life story within the first hour. Nothing is more of a turn-off than someone who chatters on and on describing their life circumstances. Needless to say, don't bring up any problems, particularly financial, on the first meeting.

The ability to make good conversation is a skill, and it can be cultivated. Ask him questions about himself, his work, his life, without sounding like you're prying. If he seems reluctant to talk about a particular subject, drop it. If he's married, don't ask about his wife and family. Instead, focus on things like his taste in music or movies, or sports, or whatever you may have discovered interests him. Be careful with current events, as you could walk into some controversial minefield of disagreement.

As important as the *what* is the *how*: listen attentively. Ask follow-up questions. Make eye contact. Show you're interested with body language as well as verbal responses.

If he's a skilled conversationalist, or a natural *mensch*, he'll ask you about yourself. Keep it light. It's okay to share some personal information, but don't get too intimate right away. You want to maintain an element of mystery. Nothing is more of a turn-off than revealing everything about yourself without nuance or room for ambiguity. Mystery fires his imagination. Mystery keeps him coming back to find out more.

If that sounds like game-playing – well, yes, there is definitely an element of playfulness in most male-female dynamics. But this isn't the kind of game-playing calculated to control or manipulate the other person; this is harmless fun. I'm talking about playfulness and flirting. I'm talking good old-fashioned common sense that wise women, goddesses, and femmes fatale have been practicing for centuries. There's a fine line between signaling interest and presenting a bit of a challenge. Yes, it's tricky to pull it off, but that midpoint is the place where you want to be.

The Life of the Mind

Forget the old stereotype about men preferring bimbos to smart women. Marilyn Monroe's biggest secret was her braininess. The truth is, most SDs want Sugar Babies to be more than just pretty shells. Some men even say there's nothing sexier than a woman's mind, and that the most erogenous zone is the one between the ears.

I'm going to assume if you're reading this that you're no dummy, but just in case you've neglected the intellectual side of life…try to read a newspaper once in awhile and keep up on social issues. Read books, from World literature to Business, and magazines, like the Economist – read everything. Develop informed opinions. Listen to people who know more than you do. Be interesting and creative.

Above all, know who you are, and that you are unique. There's only one person in the world exactly like you. If you cultivate the self-confidence born of deep inner knowledge, others will be attracted to you. The authentic Sugar Daddy has a lot to give you, and he wants a lot in return. The same goes for the authentic Sugar Baby: you have a lot to give, and you want – and deserve – a lot in return. Carry this knowledge in the back of your mind always, and you're sure to find the right Sugar Daddy and your ideal arrangement.

BEFORE AFTER

SUGAR DADDY MAKEOVER

CHAPTER SIX:

GET READY, DADDY!

As her Sugar Daddy, one of my roles is to ensure my Sugar Baby is financially secure and doesn't have to worry about finances.

— From the SeekingArrangement.com blog

The previous chapter detailed the preparations Sugar Babies should make before embarking on the search for a Sugar Daddy. Don't skip over it because it's directed at females: you just might learn something! Besides, some of the same advice applies to Sugar Daddies as well – figuring out your innermost thoughts, determining what you want from an arranged relationship, and sprucing yourself up for the hunt.

Obviously, that last item won't be quite as much of a production as it is for a Babe, since most men don't spend as much time and energy – *and money!* – on grooming. Anyhow, good looks aren't the main thing you're offering here; money is. Still, while money might be a Sugar Daddy's most important asset, it doesn't mean your looks won't affect your chances with Sugar Babies – so don't just pass right by the grooming step.

Remember, you're competing with hundreds of other Sugar Daddies, and let me tell you, a lot of the guys on the site are hot, hunky, and handsome. When Sugar Baby meets you for the first time, you can throw a hundred gee's across the table at her, but if your hair's unkempt or you're dressed in rags, it won't do you a bit of good. Like most relationships, these arrangements really get going when the chemistry's right – no matter what else happens on a date, if two people have a chemical attraction, they're going to want to see each other again. Chances are, if you look like a slob, chemistry won't happen.

I told the Babies, and now I'm telling you without beating around any bushes, this lifestyle is not usually about romantic love and its attendant rituals; this is *barter*. You are exchanging your money for services that only a beautiful, polished woman can provide. It isn't *only* about money and beauty, but during the seeking phase, these are of paramount concern.

I emphasize this because I've noticed a bit of confusion on the part of some men as to exactly what a Sugar arrangement is. More than a few Sugar Babies have met men on SD/SB websites with no previous

Sugar Daddy experience, who seem to be clueless, especially when it comes to candid discussion of financial terms. Some even get offended if a Sugar Baby truthfully states her financial needs, thinking she's mercenary or manipulative.

Listen up, guys: Putting her needs out on the table in a direct and honest way is about as far from manipulative as it gets. You might be judging Sugar Babies based on bad experiences with conventional dating, where it's common for women to try and wheedle cash and gifts out of men. TV sitcoms portray male-female relationships in these mercenary terms; think of Lucy scheming to get money out of Desi (though Lucy was more often scheming to get herself on stage!).

Here are a few words on this topic from an exemplary Sugar Daddy.

> I like helping someone out in a way that's much more exciting than just being a "good Samaritan." I encourage any SB with a compelling story to make it clear up front whatever her situation is and what she's hoping to find. That said, there's a high risk of SBs taking advantage of SDs. But this is true in all aspects of life and money. There's obviously risk on both sides.

Yes, some Sugar Babies – male *and* female – can be mercenary. Some are even running scams. A few are professional escorts or plain old-fashioned hookers, exploiting websites like SeekingArrangement to reel in wealthy customers. Horror stories about grifters posing as Sugar Babies are common, but they're outnumbered by stories of sex-crazed, con-artist, or just plain clueless Sugar Daddies. Posers have been known to jeopardize women's safety – for instance, by flying a Sugar Baby halfway across the world to meet him without providing her a ticket home.

In other words, lies and deception can and do occur on both sides of the Sugar Bowl.

But just as there are generous, authentic Sugar Daddies online, there are hundreds of beautiful, charming, sexy, and sincere Sugar Babies. People seeking arrangements simply have to be alert, and learn to distinguish the Sugar from the Splenda. We'll return to the subject of precautions later on; for now, let's review the preparations a potential Sugar Daddy should make before he begins any serious hunting expedition.

First of all, it's essential to determine what your budget is and how much you can or want to spend. Ask yourself how much disposable or discretionary income you have to spend on a Sugar Baby each month. I'm assuming you're an authentic Sugar Daddy who's financially savvy and can figure out a budget without my help.

In addition to *how much* you'll spend, you also need to think about *how* – how will you handle the financial aspect of an arrangement? Will you take her out shopping once a month? Will you give her a monthly allowance? A credit card? Pay her rent or bills? Help her with tuition, her business, or any other unusual expenses?

> Best thing I ever did with a SB that I really trusted was to give her a weekly allowance and use of a credit card. The allowance was established after about a month, based on information she gave me about her expenses. After six months, I gave her a credit card with a certain line extended, and she never violated the terms. We never had to discuss money or her financial needs ever again. That worked perfectly for me, and I'm sure it did for her also.

As important as *how much* and *how*, it's also a good idea to examine your *attitudes* around money. How do you feel giving it away? Proud and magnanimous? Resentful? Are you naturally generous?

Or do you monitor every dime? What are your feelings towards those in need, sometimes even desperate need, of money? Do you judge them? Think they're scatter-brained or losers? Do you have an understanding of the big picture and the reasons why women frequently have less money than men?

You need to face these questions so you don't carry a lot of negative baggage about money into a Sugar relationship. Some men only *think* they want to be Sugar Daddies, but when it gets down to the wire, they're ambivalent, and they do things like criticize the way Sugar Baby spends *their* money. Or they resent what they see as payment for sex.

Earlier in this book we addressed this issue of pay-per-boink, or Sugar relationships versus prostitution, pointing out how they differ. You want to be sure you have this straight in your head. If all you want is NSA sex once in a while, a hooker is cheaper and easier than keeping a Sugar Baby contentedly humming – but you wouldn't get nearly as much out of the experience. As they say, you get what you pay for in life.

You want to avoid being blindsided by emotions like resentment and anger, as they can poison any relationship. Far too many marriages are eroded by hidden resentment; wouldn't it be ironic (and sad) if your Sugar arrangement turned into something like a bad marriage?

So take a moment to consider that, in negotiating this kind of arrangement, you are using your hard-earned cash to obtain intimacy. How do you feel about that? Do you take a coolly logical view of it as just the way things are? Or even better, as a positive thing? Or will it make you feel badly about yourself? On the other extreme, you don't want to become arrogant and conceited just because you can afford the finest grade of Sugar on the market!

When you register on SeekingArrangement.com, you'll be writing up a profile of yourself, so while preparing for your Sugar search, it's a good idea to keep this profile in the back of your mind. It's the first impression of you that Sugar Babies get. Many potential partners won't respond to generalized profiles that don't give out enough information, so the more specific you can be, the better. We'll go into online profile creation in greater detail in Chapter Seven. For now, I suggest that you sit down with a pen and two sheets of paper, and at the top of the first one write *What I Want From A Sugar Baby Arrangement*, and on the second sheet, *What I Have to Offer a Sugar Baby*.

Under the first heading, write down all the reasons why you want a Sugar relationship. Is it simply fun and adventure you're after? An escape from the stresses of your life? Comfort? On-call animal lust NSA? All of the above? Be precise. This list will be useful when you do your online profile, and also when it's time to negotiate the terms of an arrangement.

Somewhere on this list be sure to include, if you didn't already, answers to these key questions:

- How often do you want to meet?
- Do you want the relationship to include sex? How often?
- Do you want your SB to be monogamous, or can she have other lovers? You?
- Do you want your SB to accompany you to social events?
- Do you want your SB to travel with you?
- Will you want her to cook for you?

- On dates, will you spend the night, or leave before morning?
- Do you want a SB who lives nearby, or out of town?
- Do you care if she has kids?
- Does the relationship need to be discreet?

When you've completed the first page, go on to the next one, writing down what you have to offer a Sugar Baby, besides money. Will you take her traveling? Be a mentor and provide financial guidance? Make her laugh? Great sex? Great conversation? Great food? Friendship? Don't be shy, but don't brag, either. Think pragmatically: which attributes of yours might give another person pleasure? For example, you might write, "handsome," or "sophisticated" or "genius with cars." (Don't laugh – I know a lot of vehicle-challenged women who'd rather have a mechanic on retainer than a lawyer!) Try to look at your assets and flaws without judging them, but if you see something you don't like, decide if you want to or can change it.

As I reminded Sugar Babies, you don't *have* to do all this work – but if you're serious about achieving your goals, then the way you go about it should be equally serious. As mentioned earlier, you're competing with hundreds of other Sugar Daddies – and if you want to attract the cream of the crop, you'd better know what makes you stand out from the crowd.

Finally, spend some time thinking about the kind of Sugar Daddy you are or want to be. How do you imagine your SD self? As a friendly companion, or a man with a mistress? Or something in between these two extremes? (We'll go into the most common types of Sugar Daddies in Chapter Nine.)

Take your time with all this. You might even want to spread it out over a few days, so you can "background process" while at work, in the shower, or in your dreams. It's well worth the time: if you're confident about who you are and what you want, you'll have a much better shot at creating your ideal arrangement.

WARNING: The following material may be hard on the heart and is not recommended for those who scare easily.

As promised: the horror segment of our program. The following are a few SeekingArrangement.com blog posts from disgruntled Sugar Daddies:

> I've had trouble getting potential SBs to follow through. I've purchased several round trip airline tickets only to experience no-shows. I don't understand why someone would let you buy them a ticket and not show up.
>
> • • • • •
>
> After a few texts today I got a note from my potential SB saying she needs $1,000 to pay off loans...{The next day}...She all but demanded the $1K, saying she couldn't wait even until Sunday to discuss it. I met this woman 3 days ago and only once in person, and she demands that I come up with $1K right now to prove I'm legitimate. If she needs money this fast and this badly then she's not a SB, she's something else.
>
> • • • • •
>
> I had one SB who took an allowance advance and then disappeared. Another one gave me an IM account, and it turned out she was just promoting her webcam business.

The scams are many, and easy to miss. How do you separate the real Sugar Babies from the down-and-dirty gold-diggers who approach men, as blues musician Taj Mahal put it, *with a handful of gimme*?

Forgive me if I'm being repetitive, but *you must pay attention!* It is not impossible to spot a scam or a pro, but you'll have to be looking at her with eyes wide open. You can't afford to get swept off your feet early on. Not that your search has to be done under a perpetual cloud of suspicion – but at the very minimum you should maintain a healthy dose of disbelief.

A Few Specifics to Watch For

- In her email correspondence, does her grammar and spelling imply an educational level other than what she's indicated? While typos and grammatical errors are common in email, you should be able to tell the difference between cyber casual and under-educated (cut her some slack if English is her second language).

- Does she contradict herself, giving out information that differs from one conversation to the next? For instance, did she say she's divorced, then in another message say she's never been married?

- Does she pre-time your date down to the minute, ask for per-date payment (rather than an allowance or gift), and refuse to commit to an ongoing arrangement? These are all the marks of a professional.

- Does she say she is from the U.S. but is currently stuck overseas and needs to be bailed out? Does she claim to need gas money in order to drive to meet you because she's afraid of flying?

- Does she say you're The One, and tell you how much she loves you after just one or two conversations? Those are all classic Internet scams, so beware!

- Does she ask for a fairly large sum of money right away, and insist she needs it in a day or two? Does she *demand* money rather than negotiate for it? Again, from the SA blog:

I was going to meet up with an SB who lives two hours away, until she demanded $1,000 for an evening together. I noticed her pictures looked like those of an escort...guys know what I'm talking about: her face either covered with hair or blurry, while her body is shown off. So I checked a couple of escort sites in her town, and guess what? Yup, there she was.

Some Do's and Don'ts

- Don't drink alcohol, at least not more than one or two, on a first date, since alcohol clouds clarity (even though it sometimes feels just the opposite).

- Don't give out your cell phone number before getting to know someone.

- If you're seriously interested but iffy about someone, consider running a background check; many online sites do them for a fee. You can get tax records, criminal background information, any marriages/divorces, past addresses, etc.

- Never send money if the relationship is long-distance, at least in the beginning. Some SDs have sent money to SBs and never heard from them again.

- When you register on SeekingArrangement.com, visit and read the blog, where Sugar Daddies unload horror stories and sometimes name names.

- You might want to register at the higher membership level on SeekingArrangement, the Diamond Club of Certified Sugar Daddies, whose identities, income, and net worth are checked and pre-verified by site administrators. If you're in this elite group, Sugar Babies know that you are who you say you are, and they'll trust you during negotiations. It's not surprising that

Diamond members receive over 20 times more responses.

- Remember that men are from Mars, women are from Venus, and communicating in different languages can be hard as hell!

I hope I haven't given the impression that there aren't sincere and wonderful Sugar Babies out there, because there most definitely are. To prove that authentic Sugar Babes exist, here are a few random blog posts of SBs talking about their dates and arrangements:

> I met a potential SD last night, and had the most amazing conversation I have had in a long time with the absolutely most amazing man I have met in an even longer time. I even wanted intimacy more than he was putting out... Can't wait to see him tomorrow.
>
> • • • • •
>
> The positive experiences have definitely outweighed the negative. Last week I flew to New York, stayed in a beautiful hotel, only to find out he didn't feel a connection. So I had a nice meal, slept alone in a very comfortable bed, and flew back the next morning with $1,000 in my pocket...because he was a wonderful, honest, and sincere man.
>
> • • • • •
>
> On my third date with my Sugar Daddy, he took me out on his boat and let me drive it....a great experience. We had a picnic and sailed around. That was the day I decided we would suit each other very well. My Sugar Daddy and I see each other once or twice every three months. I'm always stoked with excitement when he comes to town.

Here's one to break your heart:

> I had a wonderful eleven-year relationship with an older retired doctor who had a wife and grown children. Although I knew it was strictly NSA, that made it even more wonderful.

He and I went places every few months (Vegas, Tahoe, the Bahamas) but I always knew he would go home to his wife. When he found out he was ill he told me, and never contacted me again. I tried everything (within reason, keeping his secret) to contact him. Last year I spoke with his son and found out he died in January 2006. It nearly killed me. I knew I had fallen in love with him many years ago, and he knew it too. To this day, I do not nor will I ever regret that relationship. I may never share my life with someone the way my parents were able to do, but I did share the best part of myself with someone who loved me specifically for me. We never fought or argued; how many couples can say that? How many relationships have not one single bad memory? I was truly blessed. I hope I can be again someday.

And finally:

Earth-shattering, fiery sex is part of what I'm looking for! Sure, I like the cash flow, but...are there really SD's who are okay financing another life of no sex? Isn't that what wives are for?

Speaking of earth-shattering, fiery sex...the Safe Sex Police are popping by with a commercial: You should practice safe sex until and unless your arrangement becomes monogamous. Even if you know you're virus-free, she may not be. You should not only initiate safe sex procedures, you should respect her if she brings it up first. But you knew all this, didn't you?

Additionally, you should respect any precautions a Sugar Baby might take, especially at the first few meetings. Unless you've been living in a cave in Uzbekistan, I'm sure you're aware that women are too often victims of violence; meeting a stranger is statistically a greater risk for women than it is for men. Most Sugar Babies will ask to meet in a public place the first or first few times. If you set up a long-distance date or meeting, she might ask for specs on the reservations ahead of time so she can verify them. Her cell phone might ring at odd times with friends checking to be sure she's safe. *Do not take any of this personally!* These precautions aren't an indication of your character or of how she regards you, so don't take offense. Don't tease her either, or act as if she's neurotic. Considering the world we live in, she's only being sensible – so admire Sugar Baby for having the smarts to watch out for herself.

Grooming for the Sugar Bowl

This isn't exactly breaking news, so I don't think anyone will be insulted when I say that women pay more attention to grooming and hygiene than men. When it comes to improving and/or maintaining one's physical appearance, mileage varies – some men are as meticulous as women, while others think a weekly swipe with a washcloth is sufficient.

Wherever you fall on the grooming intensity scale, remember this: To a majority of women, *cleanliness matters*. Nothing turns a woman off faster than bad breath, green tooth gook, hanging nose hair, or bad odors emanating from any part of the body. Some women do become aroused by the natural smell of the male body – sexy pheromones unmasked by deodorant, not stinky poo – but until you know this is true of a specific woman, it's best to play it safe: make sure the only aroma coming off your skin is that of fresh soap (achieved by taking a shower beforehand). It's also best to avoid strong cologne or after-shave, since some people are allergic, or just might not like a particular brand.

Take stock of your appearance, using the checklist below:

- [ ] Head Hair: Length, style, smell; use dandruff shampoo if needed.
- [ ] Teeth: Get them professionally cleaned every six months. Brush twice daily.
- [ ] Breath: Brush your tongue. Use mouthwash.
- [ ] Facial Hair: Trim beard, mustache, eyebrows.
- [ ] Skin: Facials and skin care products are not for women only anymore.
- [ ] Nails: They should be scrupulously clean and filed smooth.
- [ ] Hands: Also scrupulously clean; if red and rough, use men's moisturizer.
- [ ] Body Hair: If necessary, buy nose and ear hair clippers and use them.

Regarding hairy backs and shoulders: if you saw *The 40-Year-Old Virgin*, you've probably been scared off waxing forever. Not having any first-hand experience in this area, I don't know how realistic that torture scene was, or if the process is as brutal as depicted. I do know that men with an abundance of fur use the same professionals as women do for unwanted hair removal.

Caveat emptor: The woman with whom I saw *The 40-Year-Old Virgin* could hardly bear to watch this scene: she mourned the chest hair, beloved by her, that was so carelessly discarded. There seem to be two kinds of women in the world – those who adore chest hair, and those who are sickened by it. My advice is, don't go ripping off your fur just yet – there's no need to turn yourself inside out for someone you haven't met, or hardly know, as the case may be.

Find a hair style that looks good on you by going to a salon, *not* to the family barber who gave you your first haircut. I know, I know: your father wouldn't be caught dead in a hair salon. But no matter how old or young you are, these are different times and a new generation.

If you're going bald, comb-overs are *O-U-T,* and for good reason: they make men look like pathetic dorks. If most of your hair is gone, a smooth-shaven dome is one option – if you have the looks for it. Another option is hair replacement, which has come a long way over the past decade. Again, see a professional for advice.

If your shaving techniques aren't quite up to snuff, get a professional shave and observe the way it's done. Or Google *shaving* and you're sure to find step-by-step instructions. If you have a mustache and/or beard, keep it neatly trimmed. Again, learn the correct way to care for facial hair yourself, or get it professionally trimmed.

If your teeth are extremely crooked, or unsightly in any way, you might want to look into cosmetic dentistry. Your smile is one of your most important physical assets; I remember an old TV show where the main character, a drop-dead gorgeous blonde cop, was always falling for guys because they had perfect teeth. The things that can be done these days to improve teeth are miraculous, and it's also less painful, with new techniques to ease the agony.

One popular twentieth-century trend is to hire a personal image consultant. If the very idea makes you laugh, go find a photo of the young Bill Gates and compare it to one of him today. When Bill finally lifted his head from the motherboard to hob-nob with the rich and famous, he realized the nerd look would take him only so far, and he hired someone to give him a makeover. What's good enough for the wealthiest man in America ought to be good enough for the average Sugar Daddy.

If you *really* can't deal with a professional makeover, at least read magazines like *Men's Health, Esquire* and *Details*. These are good sources of how-to's and other practical information. Men's magazines are also a good resource for the realm of the wardrobe. Most Sugar Babies don't expect you to wear designer clothing – but since a genuine Sugar Daddy can afford high-class clothing, whether designer-trendy or not, quality threads are an indication you're for real. And make no mistake, the savvy Sugar Baby *will* notice. Having met a Poser or two, she pays attention to such details.

On the other hand, don't go overboard trying to prove you've got the big bucks – don't, for instance, cover yourself with bling. The look you're aiming for is simple, nicely kempt, and casual.

Many men, even the rich and powerful, are sometimes intimidated by extremely beautiful women. They tend to worry they'll become tongue-tied, or say something stupid and make a bad first impression. Because conversation is very much of the moment, you can't effectively plan what to say ahead of time. You can, however, develop conversational skills.

Some Conversational Do's and Don'ts

Do:

- Ask her about herself (on email or in person).
- Before you meet, learn through email what topics interest her.

- Try to remember things she says for future conversational follow-up.
- Give her exclusive, focused attention when she's talking.
- Do the same when you're talking – and make eye contact.
- Keep up with current affairs – watch the news and read the papers.
- When she asks you about yourself, keep your responses light.
- Don't complain about your wife. Never, *never* say, "She doesn't understand me."
- Don't complain, period.
- You do want to share personal information, but don't get overly intimate right away.
- Instead of forcing her to raise the money issue, *you* bring it up. She'll appreciate it.

Don't:

- Don't go on and on. Restrain the urge to talk about yourself the whole time.
- Don't constantly turn the topic to yourself with "me too" or "I know how you feel."
- Don't lecture, advise, or act like you know all the answers.
- Don't be looking all over the room, whether either of you are talking or not.
- Needless to say, don't let your gaze wander towards other women.
- Don't *expect* sex. (*Down Boy!*) Anticipation does not lessen pleasure. You can wait.

- Don't raise the subject of sex on the first meeting – she'll think that's all you want.
- Don't be reluctant to talk about the financial aspect of the arrangement.
- Don't tell jokes or "tease" (you know: the way you used to tease your sister).

In most relationships, arranged or not, one person is almost always the pursuer to a greater degree, while the other is the pursued. Some people are more comfortable in one role or the other, and it doesn't seem to break down strictly along gender lines – some women are comfortable pursuing men, while others sit back waiting to be pursued. And vice versa.

Around the Sugar Bowl, however, it seems only logical that Sugar Babies would prefer to be pursued. They've signed on for a relationship in which they're supposed to be spoiled rotten with money, gifts, and attention, so it's common sense for them to be courted, to use an old-fashioned term.

Based on this educated guess, a Sugar Daddy would do well to assume the pursuer role in the beginning. This doesn't mean going after her with guns blazing; it means being the one to ask for dates, the one who opens negotiations of terms, who sends the first e-mail and makes the first phone call, sends flowers the morning after and calls the next night. Should you pick up signals that she's put off by this level of attention, you can always back off. Also, it's not an iron-clad rule or a permanent state of affairs, but a general guideline to be followed primarily in the early phases.

If this sounds like game-playing, let me reassure you. As I told Sugar Babies, game-playing is only damaging when it's calculated to control or manipulate another person. The pursuit "game," by contrast, is harmless, its only objective is to ease the difficulties or awkwardness of the negotiation phase, and to get things moving in the right direction. After all, *someone* has to drive! Remember, too, that *a man chases a girl until she catches him* – according to an ancient Eddie Fisher song.

Finally, the most valuable quality you can possess when embarking on this adventure is self-confidence. Nothing is so attractive to a woman, especially a Sugar Baby, as a man/Sugar Daddy who knows who he is, what he wants, how to get it – and *takes action*. Once a Sugar Baby feels safe, and if you two are right for one another, you won't have to worry anymore about preparations, conversational skills, sensitive subjects, or anything else – except lavishing attention, tangible or otherwise, on your Sugar Baby, and enjoying all the goodies she gives you in return.

CHAPTER SEVEN:

ONLINE SUGAR

Online websites are today's hot spot for Sugar Daddies, Sugar Mamas and Sugar Babies to connect. I'm not talking about general dating websites like eHarmony or match.com, but niche sites such as SeekingArrangement.com, SeekingMillionaire.com or MillionaireMatch.com, created specifically to serve the Sugar community.

Why not use a regular dating site? After all, most of them cater to a wide variety of relationship styles. When it comes to the *Sugar* lifestyle, though, there are compelling, even *essential,* reasons why it's best to use only SB/SD sites. First, the essential: some dating websites *do not allow* posts, comments, or profiles that even hint at anything resembling a financial component to a relationship. One Sugar Baby who posted on a general dating site was immediately booted off, with a polite note informing her they don't permit ads that "offer sex in exchange for money." Here's the ad in question:

> Older female artist tired of the struggle seeks solvent gent who wants a romantic partner/companion. Will perform domestic duties in kitchen and bedroom for support within context of a relationship. In other words, I'm ready to go back to the role of housewife. Impeccable credentials.

I included the above ad here, first, for a chuckle, but mainly to show that even an ad this remote from prostitution was censored; even on a liberal site like Craigslist, vigilante members report any posts that even hint at sex for money. If "Housewife" got booted, a blatant Sugar Baby ad doesn't stand a snowball's chance in hell.

Even on sites that aren't as strict, or if your ad somehow manages to fly in under the radar, a general dating website will most likely yield poor results, since you won't find that many Sugar Daddies or Babes using it. Adult dating sites such as AdultFriendFinders. com won't bring good results either, since they're used primarily by people looking specifically for X-Rated content and entertainment. It goes without saying that free dating sites don't attract authentic Sugar Daddies, except perhaps those unwilling to pay a membership fee – hardly the kind of guy most Sugar Babies want to meet.

The ratio of males to females on most general dating sites is about even. On adult sites it's more like ten to one: just as more men than women hang around porn shops and X-rated theaters, very few women show up in overtly sexual cyber spaces. On a dating site that caters specifically to SD/SB relationships, however, the ratio is (*hold onto your garters!*) just the opposite – a whopping ten women for every man.

If your sweet tooth was acting up and you had a choice between going to the supermarket or to the specialty bakery next door, which one would you choose to satisfy your craving? Would you wander up and down aisles of meat, cheese and household cleansers until you stumbled upon a few packaged cupcakes? Or would you open the door to the bakery and behold a gleaming display case chock full of buttercream-topped chocolate cakes, heart-shaped sprinkle cookies, and mounds of raspberry-filled danish?

It's the same when you crave a Sugar relationship: you'll save time and energy, and find higher quality, on a website that caters specifically to your sweet tooth. Additionally, the administrators here know the kind of privacy and screening required by their clientele, and tailor their policies appropriately. The success of top-of-the-line Sugar dating sites such as SeekingArrangement. com, MillionaireMatch.com, and SeekingMillionaire.com has been unprecedented, and they continue to attract new members at an astounding rate.

Getting started online is a simple process that takes less than five minutes. Registering on SeekingArrangement.com, for example, is pretty much the same as registering with Amazon or Google. Except for creating a profile, which we'll get to shortly, it's just a matter of following instructions and typing information into boxes. New Sugar Daddy and Mama members get a free trial period, and Sugar Babies play for free in perpetuity (just as they do in many singles clubs). Since Sugar Babies are frequently in financial need, asking them to pay a fee could defeat the site's purpose. It would inevitably reduce the number of Babes on the site, thereby limiting Sugar Daddies' choices. For this reason, anyone seeking a Sugar arrangement should think twice before signing on with a service that doesn't welcome Sugar Babies *gratis.*

As noted, the profile is the one time-consuming aspect of registering – which is why we're going to spend the bulk of this chapter on it. In the two preceding chapters, if you followed the instructions, you spent a fair amount of time preparing yourself for this task. It's going to pay off now, when you assemble a killer profile, your ticket to an ideal arrangement and life. (If you were a naughty Baby or Daddy and didn't do your homework, go back and do it now. Otherwise, proceed at your own risk!)

Writing a good profile is part science and part art. It's a skill you'll want to master, since a well-written profile will attract the people who best suit your requirements. Just as your résumé is a marketing tool for a job hunt, your profile is a marketing tool for your relationship hunt. And just as you can alter your résumé to suit a particular job, if you find that your profile isn't bringing home the Sugar, you can always go back and tweak it later on.

I recommend you go online now and pull up SeekingArrangement. com's profile form; you might even want to print it out. One of the most important parts of your profile is the heading – this is what everyone browsing on the site sees before anything else. It's what inspires them to click and look at your profile – or not! It had better be strong, eye-catching, and as self-descriptive as possible. I concede that making up three or four words strong enough to catch someone's interest, yet not so strong they turn someone off, and that describe you to some extent, is not the easiest task imaginable!

The most important thing about the heading is that it inspire people to click open your profile. If you have a really catchy, intriguing phrase, it doesn't necessarily matter if it describes you or not. Let's look at a few headings, good and bad.

The Good:

Sexy woman wants to be taken care of
AfroQueen searching for Vanilla King

These two are specific. While the first one could probably describe almost any Sugar Baby, the fact that she chose *sexy* says a lot about her; ditto that she wants *to be taken care of.*

Rare slender elegant beauty
Open to suggestions

While these two aren't terribly descriptive, they are intriguing. Every word in the first heading is evocative; it calls to mind definite associations. The second heading is a little risqué, a little bit cute; enough to make someone curious enough to click.

First Class ticket to dimensions within dimensions – someone looking for a deep, spiritual, Sugar Baby would probably click on this.

Healthy, Wealthy and Wise Seeks Down To Earth Girl – This is descriptive, it tells you this guy is older, and it lets you know what kind of woman he wants.

Looking to spoil you
Looking for a Girl to Spoil Weekly
Can I spoil you?

Any Sugar Daddy heading that uses the word spoil is excellent – it lets the ladies know you're serious and experienced with Sugar arrangements.

Seeking partner in crime – When in doubt, use humor! This might not tell you much about the Sugar Daddy – except that he has a sense of humor, and that counts for a lot. I'll bet more people, male and female, click on something humorous than on any other kind of heading.

The Bad:

Single Young Student
Let's see if this works
Gentleman seeking a lady
Shhhhh!!
Good times ahead
It's now or never! :)
I'm the one!!!!
European girl
Houston Hottie
Sassy but classy

Every one of these headings is vague, so much so that I bet you can't even guess the gender of some of them. They tell nothing about the person or what he or she wants, and they in no way reveal personality. Some of them are even silly.

Turn-Offs:

Hey Boys, does anbody wanna....
Cum here Daddy...I need a spankin'!!!
"Oooooo do u kno how 2 handle that weapon?"

Maybe I'm wrong; maybe the male love for all things sexual will inspire lots of clicking on these headings. If so, let's just hope these Sugar Babies mean it – this kind of advertising might attract a lot more than they bargained for.

On the other end of the spectrum:

Looking to make new friends

WTF? Is this guy for real? Did he really join SeekingArrangement to make a lot of friends? Besides sounding false, most Sugar Babies would probably be turned off by the idea that Sugar Daddy's looking for multiple gals right from the get go.

I hope these examples help you to write a dynamite heading for your profile.

Moving along: notice that there are two more places on the form that call for more than a word or two: the Descriptions. The first is where you'll describe yourself, the second for describing the kind of person and/or relationship you want.

The main objectives of the profile are to introduce yourself, make a good first impression, and attract specific kinds of people. Keep these objectives in mind when creating your profile, and follow these four general guidelines:

Be Honest. Some people assume that to make a good first impression you must present yourself in glowing, one hundred percent positive terms. While you naturally want to emphasize your best qualities, going overboard will more likely arouse suspicion than attraction. Most importantly, if you present yourself as what you are *not*, potential partners who respond to your invented persona will inevitably be disappointed, and the first meeting is apt to be the last. Additionally, you might attract people that aren't exactly who you want to meet, since they're not responding to *you*, but to someone you made up. Thus, in the interests of the big picture – creating your ideal arrangement – it's highly recommended you tell the truth in your profile, the whole truth and nothing but the truth, so help you god.

Be Thorough. A one-sentence description of yourself isn't going to cut it. Both Sugar Daddies and Sugar Babies complain, on the blog, about profiles that are too general, too brief, or hopelessly vague. Think about it: would you respond to a profile that gave you hardly any information about the person? Unless accompanied by a photo that knocked your socks off, why would you bother? After all, you can always move on to one that's more intriguing.

Remember, online you're competing with hundreds of people. Sugar Babies in particular face intense competition, what with approximately ten of them for every Sugar Daddy on the site – which, by the way, doesn't mean Sugar Daddies get their "pick of the litter" without working for it: there may be a lot of Babes on the site, but women tend to be choosy. You don't have to write a full biography; if you include the right details, three or four paragraphs in each description area should do nicely.

Sugar Babies: Since you'll be posting a picture along with your profile, there's no need to describe your looks; don't waste time and words on it.

Sugar Daddies: For privacy reasons, some men don't post pictures, and therefore might want to describe themselves – briefly. *Very briefly*. What, after all, does your height and eye color tell someone? I've found that most people resemble at least one other person in the world, so if you liken yourself to a celebrity that everyone knows, it'll make it a lot easier to visualize you – but only if you *really do* resemble that person. (Don't say you're a dead ringer for George Clooney unless you are; Sugar Baby would be within her rights to sue you for cruel and unusual treatment.)

Sugar Daddies: A word about the item that says: **My Budget**. As noted in Chapter Four, this means **the amount of disposable income you have each month, after expenses, to spend on a Sugar Baby.** While you can enter "Open – Negotiable," it's better to be specific. Entering a dollar figure says you're serious, and it gives Sugar Babies more information.

Sugar Babies: In the space that says *I Expect*, you're supposed to specify the amount of money you'd like a Sugar Daddy to give you on a regular basis. If you want a regular allowance, and you know how much, fill in that number. This isn't the place to low-ball or be shy; by expecting a regular monthly allowance, you'll attract the Sugar Daddies who can afford and want to give it.

Some women don't actually "expect" a cash allowance, but are more interested in gifts, travel, visits to the spa, an occasional bailout, etc. In that case, it's best to enter the lowest figure rather than leaving it open to negotiation; as stated, specificity is always better, and besides, it's not as if you expect nothing.

The most important part of the profile is who you are and what makes you tick. Is there something unique that sets you apart from others? What are your best traits? Your likes and dislikes? Favorite ball team/music/ice cream/movie? Defining life experiences? Pivotal changes you've undergone? An unusual family history (no violence or heavy dysfunction at this point)? Values and beliefs that are important to you? Endearing quirks? Talents or gifts? Any of these, plus your own ideas along these lines, can make for an interesting profile. They give the reader something substantial to hang onto, as well as potential points of connection. If someone likes the same kind of music as you do, they're bound to respond. One rabid Yankee fan *will* email another (just remember, saying this will automatically screen out Red Sox fans).

Be Specific. Clearly describe what you're looking for in another person and in an arrangement. Be polite in the way you express yourself, but tell it like it is. The more details you provide, the better your chances of attracting someone who fits the bill. If you simply cannot abide skinny men, then say you prefer a muscular build. If your dates will have to tolerate a quirk or habit of yours – smoking is a good example – mention it. You *want* to rule out anyone who won't tolerate it, rather than waste time and energy with messages and phone calls, only to have the whole thing go up in smoke the first time you light up.

If you want a Daddy who'll help pay your tuition, say so. If you want a Sugar Baby to be your personal assistant, spell it out. By being specific, you'll attract people who want what you're offering, thereby saving everyone's time.

On the other hand, you don't want to blab so much about yourself that there's nothing left for the other person to discover.

Also, you don't want to scare someone off with anything that could be misinterpreted. Here's a good way to decide whether to put something questionable into your profile: if you absolutely feel that a person *must* have some personality trait or asset in order for you to consider them – or *lack* some trait or other – that's a deal-breaker for you, then you should definitely mention it. For instance, if you're a committed Democrat who can't stand talking to Republicans (or vice versa), that's a deal-breaker.

The same goes for anything about yourself that you want someone to know before meeting you. If you're awkward on the phone, for instance, you might want people to know it, so they don't write you off if your first phone conversation is less than scintillating.

In summary, besides including lively, fun, and interesting details in your profile, you should put in any deal-breakers and vital facts. Anything not so important that it can wait for a meeting or even later...well, it can wait.

Be Charming. Everyone loves to laugh, and everyone likes a sense of humor. So try to inject humor into your profile. If wit doesn't come naturally to you, don't agonize or try to force it; if you do, it will sound forced. But if you can manage to come up with something even slightly amusing, use it. Beware too much self-deprecation: a little bit is fine, but too much of it can get tedious and seem self-hating after awhile. Remember, this is a first impression. *You* know yourself, and *you* know what you're saying with your words – but readers will take them at face value. So don't be ambiguous or use *double entendres* at this stage; you can always show off your impressively complicated wit after you've met. For now, keep it light and amusing.

The Photo

Profiles with at least one photograph receive five to ten times more responses than those without any. For this reason, uploading one or more photos of yourself is highly recommended. That said, a badly taken picture can do more harm than good, so make sure the photo you choose is a good one. But what exactly is a "good" photo?

A good photo presents a positive side of you – your whimsical style, confident posture, or seductive good looks. Additionally, a good photo is clear, not blurry or too light or too dark; your face should be clear, the features distinct. Don't use a picture taken from a distance that hardly shows your face, unless it's a second or third photo. Yes, some people post more than one – a close-up, a full-body shot, and a profile make for a fairly complete presentation.

If you're one of those people who's un-photogenic (you know who you are), you might consider hiring a professional to do a shoot, taking an array of different poses and letting you choose from among the proofs. Or you might want to go to the mall and get a set of glamour pictures done. If you're unsure about a picture, ask a trusted friend for an opinion. *Caveat:* If someone else likes a photo of you but you still hate it, *do not use it.* It's not the way you want to be seen, and that's what counts.

Don't use a decades-old photo that shows you with a full head of hair long since gone, or with not a wrinkle on your brow. Needless to say, don't use someone else's picture. Either of these ploys will only cause disappointment when someone actually meets you.

And remember, that old cliché is true: *One picture is worth a thousand words.*

To illustrate what's been covered so far, the following are a few random bits from profiles, along with commentary. (For privacy reasons, I'm not posting entire profiles, so don't judge them as if they were.)

The Good:

> I smoke and have kids and I'm almost forty! There, that eliminated about four thousand eight hundred and thirty-seven wasted conversations! I like to shoot pool, play loud music, tell dirty jokes and dance. I am a flirt, tho not a sl*t. I am sarcastic, cynical and believe half of what I see and none of what I hear. I make friends easily. I say really bad words sometimes. I'm turned on by men who give me attention and who know how to shop.

I wonder if you can tell why I consider this a good description? No? I won't keep you guessing...What I find excellent about it is the way the writer's personality shines through. We don't just learn that she likes to dance; we also find out, on a visceral level, that she's funny, energetic, and a hoot to be with. Further, she puts potential Sugar Daddies on notice with "who know how to shop."

> I am seeking someone that would enjoy visiting me periodically in S--, and traveling to exotic places.

It's fairly obvious what's good here: it's simple and specific. Yes, there should be more detail, like who's paying, whether travel will be first class or student hostel all the way, how often...still, it's not uncommon for an SD to want a travel companion only, and from this description, a Sugar Baby knows the limits. It's possible for a SB to have one Sugar Daddy to take her traveling, and another one, or even two, who meet her other needs – just as long as all parties involved are okay with these arrangements.

> US$3,001 – $5,000 monthly
> Description: As a writer, the perfect arrangement for me
> would be one that provided for my living and marketing
> needs. I want to work away from home less, to travel
> and promote my books more. I can take care of the spe-
> cial needs of that special man extremely well. We would
> definitely have to have some chemistry. I don't have a
> problem making a commitment, if desired.

I included the amount of allowance this Sugar Baby asked for, which is on the high end, since it makes sense in the context of her description. She's blunt without being rude, clearly states her needs, mentions a willingness to reciprocate, and includes a *caveat* that the chemistry has to work. This Sugar Baby, by the way, was just as thorough in describing herself, and she posted three photos. All told, that's a good profile.

Good/Bad (has elements of both):

> I am a good-looking healthy 45-year-old. I have worked
> hard and acquired all the trappings, big house, boats,
> a plane, etc. I have also been knocked around enough
> to know these things are of no value without the right
> person to share them with. I'm looking for a young, fun,
> caring, beautiful blond blue-eyed girl. I am open to any
> kind of arrangement. If we meet, I will be charming and
> you will have a great time.

This man is specific about who he is and the kind of woman he wants – but he's not too sure about the arrangement. Notice I'm not calling him a Sugar Daddy: the terminology of Sugar dating doesn't apply. This man would probably do better on a conventional dating site. On the other hand, maybe he's heard about the Sweet Life, and he's curious to find out more about it. That's fine for him, but any Sugar Baby hell-bent on an allowance and other perks would be better off looking elsewhere. This is the kind of guy who confuses Sugar Babies. Because he doesn't know how things work in Sugarland, he might be put off when he realizes what Sugar Babies expect from him. He might judge them as bad or wrong for it.

Listen up, guys: If you don't know anything about being a Sugar Daddy, but you're curious and you want to find out, do a little homework before you go plunging into the Sugar Bowl. Read the blog. Read this book and anything else you can get your hands on about the Sugar lifestyle. Seek out and talk to people who live it. Don't start dating before you at least understand the rules and the structure. Most important, don't lay any trips on the women you meet on a Sugar site. Even if you feel judgmental, keep it to yourself.

The Bad:

My Budget: Open – Amount Negotiable
Description: Uncomplicated, fun, sexy friendship

Not only isn't this Sugar Daddy forthcoming with his budget, but his description of the woman – or is it the relationship he's looking for? – is vague.

I'm 5'6, blue eyes, curvy but on the heavy side, if u would like to know more then please contact me
I'm Seeking:
 Sugar Daddy
I Expect:
 US$1,000 – $3,000 monthly
Description: n/a

All you Sugar Daddies out there, aren't you just *dying* to contact this babe? She's heavy, has blue eyes, wants a hefty monthly allowance, and doesn't care who you are or what you look like. *Nuff said.*

And finally, can you guess what's wrong with this picture?

> I have so many people I have to keep happy but no-body seems to care if I'm happy. I haven't been happy in a long time but nobody notices. They still expect me to care about their stuff even if they don't care about mine. That's why I'm looking for a Sugar Daddy, to have someone I can talk to, someone who will try to make me happy instead of always expecting me to make him happy.

I feel for this Sugar Babe, I really do. But she should see a counselor or a therapist, or talk to a friend, instead of dumping online. It's unlikely that a good arrangement can develop from this kind of beginning. Worse, she's made herself vulnerable to those who prey upon poor lost souls – sadly, such people exist everywhere. Nobody has to play Pollyanna or fake a state of delirious happiness, but a little less self-pity and a little more giving might attract someone who eventually *will* care about her, and maybe even improve her sad life. As written, her profile dooms her to even more depression.

International Arrangements

A few words about international arrangements: it's a good idea to play only with Sugar Babes and Daddies close to home. People from all over the world can tell a convincing hard-luck story, and start picking your pocket before the ink is dry on the dinner check. I don't mean to be xenophobic, and I'm not saying that Americans don't scam with equal aplomb – it's just that someone who lives on the other side of the planet can disappear with greater ease. Also, people from desperately poor countries purposely target American men as easy marks; when they discover the Sugar phenomenon, it becomes just another trick in their repertoire.

From that statuesque Nigerian you've been writing for nearly a month comes an overseas phone call: she went home to attend her father's funeral without letting you know, and is stranded in a five-star hotel with a gargantuan bill. *Quick, send money!* From Russia with not much love comes an overnight letter from the lonely beauty trying so hard to come see you: she needs financial help to get to Moscow for a visa. Two days after you wire the money, she calls again and says she was robbed, and is stuck in Moscow with nowhere to stay. *Quick, send more money!*

Some of these con artists might even have connections to organized crime, and these days crime is global: more groups than those familiar Mafiosi operate on American shores now. There's the Russian mob, African gun-runners, and teenage gangsters of all ethnicities; pirates on the ocean, terrorists in the air, and smugglers on the road, who drag their wretched human cargo all over the planet. Considering the potential risks, when it comes to relationships that involve an exchange of money, it would be prudent to heed *West Side Story's* musical warning and *Stick to your own kind/One of your own kind.*

Phase Email, or, Let the Pursuit Begin

After you put up your profile, including photos, turn off your computer and forget about it (I know, easier said than done). Wait two or three days – that's about how long it should take to get a nibble or two. The next step in this process is responding to people who send you messages, and starting up email correspondences with them.

Email is like no other form of person-to-person contact in the history of human communication. While it resembles letter-writing, it's completely different. It isn't just a faster mode, it's more immediate, verging on the pace of talk – only it *isn't* talk. I'm not the first person to notice that email is unique, and requires unique skills. Here are some general email tips:

- Never use e-mail to "let off steam". Take a deep breath, and wait half a day.
- Set a five or ten-minute "don't send rule." Save messages in your drafts folder. You'll be surprised how well you'll be able to revise a poorly written message when you go back to it.
- Frequent emoticons, chain jokes, and smiley faces say "Don't take me seriously."
- Use spell-check. Mangled sentences and typos make you seem careless or even uneducated.
- Don't abbreviate.
- Don't inundate someone by sending them three messages at once.
- Listen to me! Using a lot of exclamation points makes you seem childish!! Don't do it!!!!
- ALL CAPS IS FOR SHOUTING!
- Be considerate: don't add unnecessary attachments, signature graphics, disclaimers, html coding, cute quotes and icons – especially dancing icons.

The question of who makes first contact is a touchy one. Some people believe the male "*should*" be the first; others think it doesn't matter. Earlier I spoke about the pursuer and the pursued, and how people seem to settle into one of these roles fairly early in a relationship. As I pointed out, it's logical that Sugar Babies would want to be the pursued; thus, a Sugar Daddy can't go wrong making the first contact.

Now that the pursuit has begun, how long should the email phase last? Some people, primarily women, prefer to prolong this phase before moving on to the phone or meeting. Others, primarily men, consider email a tool for setting up a phone or in-person date. These gender differences make sense: after all, email is a little bit like foreplay. It follows that Sugar Daddy would be wise to accommodate the Sugar Baby who wants to linger in cyberspace. Three to five message cycles is probably about right; that's enough time to ask a few questions, do a little flirting, and inspire anticipation without things dragging. Keeping messages going any longer than that without meeting can be risky: one or both of you might get bored, or you might even have a cyber spat.

Email correspondence seems to lend itself to misunderstanding to a greater degree than either letter-writing or phone conversation. My longest friendship came to a bitter end soon after we began emailing. I've heard of family members who email for awhile, then get into a war of words and cut off communication for months, until someone breaks down and shoots a joke into the other's mailbox, and the cycle starts up all over again. I don't know how or why this happens, but it does, so avoid potentially controversial topics. Remember too that in cyber communication, brevity is the better part of valor: less is more and shorter is longer.

Here are some do's and don'ts to help you successfully navigate the clumps and bumps of online Sugar dating.

DON'T send a form introduction to everyone on the site, or to a hundred members, or even ten. People aren't stupid; they can spot a form email no matter how much saccharine you pour into it – and most don't like it. *DO* send an individual email to each person who interests you, geared toward what you read in each individual profile.

DO communicate via the website. Spammers are always collecting email addresses on dating websites, so be smart: *DON'T* give out your personal email address until you've gotten to know someone and are certain you want them to have it.

DO be polite and courteous. Even if someone is rude to you first, it's better to break off communication than to engage in nasty repartee. People online tend to compare notes, and if you're rude, it could get around and work against you. Besides, why waste precious time and energy on bitterness, when with the click of a mouse you can have sweetness?

DO give praise if it's genuine and deserved. If you like what someone looks like, or what s/he says, and you're sincerely impressed, it's fine to say so. *DON'T* go overboard with compliments; it's bound to sound desperate.

DON'T complain or tell sad stories about your life and relationships. Again, you're addressing people who don't know a thing about you, and you don't want their first – and perhaps only – impression to be of a depressed or angry person. On the other hand, *DON'T* come off as a vapid Pollyanna, living in a marshmallow world of perfection. Just be real.

DON'T gossip or complain about people you've met or dated on the site, even though it can be tempting. What's wrong with this?

Let me count the ways! First, as with the above "don't," you'll leave an impression of being mean-spirited. Second, as already noted, people on the site compare notes. Third, the person to whom you're complaining just might know or meet up with whoever you're busily trashing. Fourth, the person will wonder if you talk about him or her the same way. I could go on...but you get the point.

DO convey a sense of yourself. After all the hard work you did in the chapter *Dipping into the Sugar Bowl*, this should be a snap! Fresh from taking a long hard look at yourself, assessing your good and bad qualities, and defining what you want out of life and relationships, revealing some of your true self in email messages should come naturally. Write from your alert, self-aware center. Take your time and review your words carefully before hitting the SEND button.

DON'T, on the other hand, inundate someone you hardly know with tons of personal information. Until you have an idea of who you're talking to, you don't know if you can trust the person. This is probably why some people want to move out of the email phase and get to the phone and a meeting sooner rather than later. But bypassing the email exchange isn't a solution; a person's email style is part of them too. It's really a highly individualized matter: only you know how much time you want to remain in email mode. Eventually you'll learn what works best for you. Remember practice makes perfect – so *DON'T* skip the practice.

DO ask lots of questions regarding someone's reasons for and experience with Sugar dating. The whole purpose of your communication is to see if an arrangement is in the cards, so questions are not only appropriate, they're expected. *DON'T* be shy; a lot of questions *must* be asked and answered in this situation.

DO start negotiating. While most negotiations will probably occur after you've met and decided to try and make a go of it, some basic information is good to know at the front end. Email is a chance to find out, at the very least, if what you want meshes with what the other person wants. There's no room – or necessity – for game-playing in the Sugar Bowl.

DON'T send money – to *anyone*. Fraud is common in the online dating world, and it's particularly easy to perpetrate on a Sugar website, what with Babes openly seeking financial help. *Daddies:* Not only shouldn't you give someone money before you've met and negotiated an arrangement, you should not send money through the mail at all, no matter what. (This was discussed earlier, in the section on protecting yourself.)

DON'T give your bank account information to strangers. *Babies:* If a Sugar Daddy asks for your bank account information so he can deposit money into it, *just say no*. Check fraud is common; even if you do get a deposit, it might not be legitimate. If you spend the money, you could receive a collection notice from your bank later on saying the deposit was fraudulent, and that you owe them the money you no longer have.

DO end it nicely when the time comes. If you decide, after one or two message cycles – or at any point – that this person isn't for you, simply thank them for their time and say you're not interested. Don't be rude. Needless to say, don't be crude either – it can get you kicked off the site.

DO understand that *NO* means *NO*. **DON'T** continue to pester someone who's ended your email communication.

DON'T take rejection personally. When someone decides not to go any further with you, recognize that s/he barely knows you, is probably in communication with several other potential mates, and could be breaking it off for any number of reasons. Maybe s/he resumed seeing an ex. Maybe a parent is dying. It might have nothing to do with you. Even if it does, so what? There's plenty more candy in the Sugar Bowl – move on!

DO try to understand the logistics of online dating. If you write to ten people, you're likely to be rejected by nine. If you've ever worked on a mail order campaign you know that a one percent rate of return is considered successful.

DON'T expect to meet your ideal partner within your first week online. *DO* expect to comparison shop. The beauty of the Internet is the ease of comparison shopping, whether you're looking for a lamp, a pair of shoes or a Sugar arrangement. The difference between a lamp and a Sugar Baby or Sugar Daddy is that the latter takes a lot longer to find, and involves more than just looking at pictures on your computer.

Finding the right arrangement is a long process. It might take a month, or it might take two years. You might go out with two potential partners, or you might go out with two dozen. But, as evidenced by what people say on the blog, it's a helluva ride getting there. You'll meet interesting people, visit new places, and have exciting adventures. The trick is to enjoy the journey as much as the destination.

Sugar and Spice

Good authors too who once knew better words
now only use four-letter words writing prose
'cause anything goes.
— Cole Porter

Man (and woman) does not survive on sugar alone. In order to capture and hold a potential lover's interest you'll need to toss an occasional dash of spice in with the sugar.

In private email correspondence, anything goes. For legal and other reasons, professional sex workers – escorts, prostitutes, etc. – are forbidden from advertising on SeekingArrangement.com and most websites, but other than that, people can say whatever they want in email messages. (Bear in mind that it's just about impossible to permanently lose or destroy anything written in cyberspace, so you might want to think twice about the footprints you leave behind.)

That said, sexual titillation and innuendo are inevitable, and add to the intrigue of online dating. It should come as no surprise that men are more enthusiastic than women about engaging in hot talk via email. Explicit sexual language from a stranger usually turns a woman off, and could even frighten her – and yet that same language turns a man on. As in all male-female interactions, compromises must be made on both sides.

Just as a woman in lingerie is often more exciting than in the nude, the merest hint of physical pleasure can be far more arousing than a page of vivid sexual description. In Hollywood love scenes, a glimpse of an actor's face during sex can be more arousing than full frontal nudity. The same is true in email correspondence: again, less is more.

Daddies: It's prudent to bide your time and let Sugar Baby refer to sex first. If you get impatient and decide to go ahead, choose your words carefully. Keep them ambiguous enough that she can ignore them if she so chooses.

Babies: Don't be too shy to tease and flirt in your emails. I hereby challenge you to go beyond innocent flirting and drop at least one unambiguous sexual remark. Don't do it in your first email of course, and maybe not in the second one either; when you choose to be suggestive will depend on how free and intimate you and SD become in your messages. By the third one you should be able to tell if hot talk will be welcomed. (Believe it or not, some guys do *not* like dirty talk. Honest.) A little bit of titillation goes a long way in cyberspace. Casually refer to yourself as hot, or sexy, or as someone who enjoys sex. Or say you're looking for someone sexy.

There's a difference between titillation and vulgarity – the trouble is, everyone has their own interpretation of which is which. *"What I like is erotica; what you like is pornography,"* goes the old saying. Better to play it safe by being subtle, even if it means that your innuendo sails right past the person's head. That's preferable to coming off crude.

Just as nobody can tell you exactly what to say in conversation, nobody else can tell you how to walk the fine line between delicious eroticism and crude vulgarity. This is an area in which you learn by doing, and the more practice you get, the easier it will become. The day you're able to drop a scintillating, sizzling hot line into an otherwise chaste note and make it sound utterly natural, that's the day you'll have mastered the art of hot talk.

In the meantime, practice, baby, *practice!*

"Why should men have all the fun?"

CHAPTER EIGHT:

SUGAR OFFLINE

In the Introduction to this book I spoke about the isolation that people living unconventional lives often experienced before the Internet connected them with one another. The lack of a central meeting place probably meant fewer people lived the Sugar lifestyle than actually wanted to. Still, those who were determined did manage to find one another. After all, people have been doing the Sugar dance, in one form or another, since time immemorial. You might want to explore some of the time-worn methods practiced by your historical foredaddies and forebabies as an adjunct to your online search. Some of the things they did, such as watching high-class boat races or lunching in ritzy country clubs, sound like great fun.

Sugar Babies found their Sugar Daddies, and vice versa, through personal ads in newspapers, by frequenting places where the wealthy tended to congregate, and by being inventive and creative. This route calls for a diligent, well-planned yet common-sense approach. The main strategy is to put yourself, as often as possible, in the path of the people you want to meet; you could almost call it stalking, but without the negative connotations usually associated with that term.

The dictionary definition of *stalk* is "to move stealthily." That's fairly benign, which is not how we tend to think of stalking. But in the hunt for a Sugar arrangement, moving stealthily is precisely what you do: you don't behave or appear desperate, and you don't rush into anything. You quietly go wherever you're likely to meet the people you want to meet. If that's stalking…well then, let the stalking begin!

Pre-Internet, a Sugar Baby went about her hunt for a Sugar Daddy with dead seriousness. Pre-feminism and the sexual revolution, there came a time in every girl's life when she focused all her wits and energy on finding a husband; the Sugar Baby did the same, except she refined her search to a specific kind of man, and with something more exotic than marriage as her goal.

Every serious endeavor begins with a plan. This goes for Sugar Daddies as well as Sugar Babies, even though we're talking more here about steering Babes toward those areas most heavily populated by Daddies. In a way, guys have a big advantage offline: Babes come looking for them, so they can just sit back and wait, at least initially.

They don't have to rearrange their lives or their activities in order to meet beautiful women.

Sugar Babes, ask yourselves this: when you imagine the ideal Sugar Daddy, where is he and what is he doing? Is he on the crowded floor of the New York Stock Exchange, wheeling and dealing? Riding his horse around his Scarsdale estate? Drinking espresso on the deck of his beachfront home in Malibu? On a long haul flight in business or first class? At a party in Beverly Hills talking to Jude Law? One thing you can be certain of: busy millionaires aren't hanging out on MySpace talking about their favorite music downloads. They don't have time – their plane leaves for Paris in two hours.

Ground Zero: Sugar Bowl USA

Millionaires live in every part of the country – and the world – but some areas of the U.S. are literal money hubs. Naturally, that's where you'll find the people who do a lot of getting and spending. (As they always say on crime shows: *Follow the money!*)

Some cities are more equal than others. Think about it: where are the seats of American power and money located? If you guessed New York, Washington D.C., Los Angeles (Hollywood), and Las Vegas, you hit the jackpot. Each of these cities is home to some big-money industry: New York is the financial center of the universe; DC is rife with politicians and the corporate players who control them; LA/Hollywood is home to the movie biz; and Las Vegas is… well, Las Vegas' industry *is* money (with the added attraction of lenient divorce laws and handy little wedding chapels standing by). Because they attract the rich and those who aspire to be, each of these cities is Ground Zero for Sugar.

That doesn't mean you should pack up all your belongings and move to one of these places; it does mean that you should plan to spend your next vacation in one of them – or, if you live close enough, go there for a day trip or a for a weekend. If you'd rather be on the beach than in the city, check out one of their annexes, such as the Hamptons in New York, or Malibu near LA. That's what I mean by a common-sense approach: whatever you happen to be doing during the course of your normal life, choose to do so in a way and a place that'll put you in contact with the wealthy. But first you'll need to identify exactly where they gather – you can't just land at Kennedy Airport and holler, "Yoo-hoo, Sugar, I'm here!"

Haunts of the Rich / Playgrounds of the Wealthy

In every city, certain bars, restaurants, and cafes are known as *the* places for *the "in" crowd*. Depending on social milieu or profession, people go to specific places to see and be seen, to network, or to wheel and make deals. Elaine's in Manhattan, for instance, has been known for decades as a late-night hangout for theater people. Michael's Pub in the East 50's, where Woody Allen regularly jams with the house band, is Monday night's must-go-to place. For sushi, entertainment people go to Nobu; for pastrami sandwiches it's the Carnegie Deli.

On Pacific Coast Highway in Malibu there's a diner where people whose names dominate the headlines go to eat breakfast. If you work in high finance or want to meet those who do, go further north, to San Francisco, and have a drink at The Top of The Mark, a cocktail lounge in the penthouse of the Mark Hopkins Hotel. The Redwood Room in the theater district is another SF "in" place, with a slightly older clientele.

Every city has its hot spots, and they're written up in magazines that cater to the elite: *Los Angeles, New York*, San Francisco's *7X7*. Go to the library and pore through back issues. Read local newspapers, especially "three-dot columns" devoted to news of the rich and famous; you'll find out who was seen where last night, who goes to which fundraisers, who hangs on which person's arm and which one's arm is currently empty. You might even find out who's likely to be where the very night you're in town. Sugar Daddies don't stand around the airport waiting for an interesting piece of luggage to pass by; nor do they just fall off the back of a truck. Do your homework.

In your daily life, begin thinking like a rich person: choose the places you go to using a new set of criteria. For instance, you probably use the dry cleaners closest to home, the one that does a great job, never lost your leather jacket, and charges reasonable prices – all of which makes good sense. From the perspective of your Sugar hunt, however, it makes better sense to take your clothes, even if you have to *schlep* across town, to the place that advertises a specialty in fur, leather, designer clothes, or – and I've only just discovered this – "Executive Shirt Service."

Here are some more ways to incorporate Sugar into your diet:

- As attached as you might be to the neighborhood coffee shop where you know everyone and everyone knows you, it's time to trade up. Start getting your caffeine hit in the Financial District, at Starbucks or another café, just so long as it's filled with suited executives reading the *Wall Street Journal*. You, on the other hand, should be reading some trendy new book on black holes in space, or charging your brain; any complex subject will do, as long as it really interests you. When is a book not a book? When it's a conversation piece.

- Take an inventory of all the places you go – bank, food markets, wine shops, home improvement stores – and do the same thing as with the coffee shop: find the most upscale version, or one located in an expensive neighborhood. Unfortunately, you'll no longer be able to dash out wearing sweats and a *schmatte* on your uncombed hair; you'll have to pay more attention to what you look like when you go out on even the most trivial errand.

- Pay attention to cars. Make a mental note of the streets or neighborhoods where you see more Rolls Royce's, Ferrari's, Porsche's or Mercedes – or private limos.

- If you're going to the mall, choose one with the most expensive stores (Neiman Marcus rather than JC Penney) located in the ritziest neighborhood.

- If you find out a technological convention is in town, see if you can go to some of the exhibits or workshops – or hang out in nearby clubs and cafes to meet wealthy techies. Too nerdy for you? Where'd you think Bill Gates came from?

- Keep your eyes peeled for other events likely to import out-of-town Sugar. For instance, if you want to meet famous buff athletes, and baseball's July All-Star Game is scheduled in your city, plan your week around it. Events subsidiary to the game include a parade, autograph signings, and a huge exhibit. In between baseball events, Derek Jeter and Alex Rodriguez have a lot of down time to fill. Find out which hotels the players are staying in and hang out in the lobbies or lounges.

- Speaking of hotel lobbies, they're terrific meeting places. The best times of day are just before meals, when everyone meets in the lobby and heads to a restaurant. Order a cocktail or coffee and sit on one of the plush sofas, reading that trendy book. *Caveat:* Hookers and upscale escorts frequent hotel lobbies; staff are hip to them and regularly throw them out. Dress conservatively and carry an upscale shopping bag or two (with something in them) so as not to be taken for a hooker.

- When flying somewhere, if you can afford it, upgrade to business class. (Some airlines let you use frequent flyer miles to upgrade.) A famous TV reporter got upgraded, when she was a college student, to Business Class, and that's where she met her Sugar Daddy.

- Attend free art gallery openings…go to wine tastings…stop in at food festivals held in urban parks on holiday weekends. Gourmet restaurants set up sampling booths at these festivals, and where there's gourmet food, there's gourmet people.

- Instead of going to a crowded singles bar for an after-work cocktail, try a lounge like The Redwood Room in San Francisco's Clift Hotel, the newly reopened Plaza Oak Bar in New York, or the swimming-pool bar of Miami's Fountainbleu.

- Looking for a new car? Yes, I know, you're headed for the Toyota dealership – but it wouldn't hurt to take a peek in the BMW showroom. Not only might you bump into a potential Sugar mate, you'll most likely get a chance to drive a Beamer. Sure, it breaks your heart to go back to the Toyota – but 'tis better to have driven and left a Beamer than never to have driven one at all. Besides, at the rate you're going, a BMW will be yours someday soon, so you might as well get familiar with it.

Cities aren't the only places to hunt for Sugar – far from it. Certain beach or golf resorts are known to attract the rich and elite – places like the Pebble Beach Golf Course in Carmel; Martha's Vineyard; Vail, Colorado or Park City, Utah for skiing. Of course, Sugar Babies will have to do some fancy finagling for places to stay, since you probably can't yet afford a house or hotel room on these sugar plantations. Then again, you don't have to actually stay overnight: you can just go for a meal or a drink.

Sailors and yachtsmen are always looking for crews – and not just chief cooks and bottle washers. They also look for beautiful women to bring along on whatever ocean voyage they're taking. This will take guts, because once you're out on the sea there's nowhere else to go if Sugar Dad turns out to be sour. You might try to get to know him some first, by finding him through an ad in a publication called *Latitude 38*. Look under the "Crew wanted" ads, *carefully*: sometimes the wording isn't as up front as it is on the Internet. Fall is a good time to begin this search, since just before Halloween the boats men descend on the marina in San Diego to organize a trip to Baja California. Even if you don't answer an ad, it's a good idea to attend the festivities in San Diego; everyone's partying on the boats, and you never know who you might meet.

Here's a bit of irony: while most people want to get *off* mailing lists, the Sugar Baby on the hunt should get *on* as many as possible – that is, on a certain class of mailing list. Make a small donation to your nephew's elite private school and you're on the list; now you'll know whenever they have an event, like their annual reception. Go to these; you'll meet the wealthier donors.

Enter your name for the door prize at an art gallery opening. Get on lists for film festivals, charity fundraisers, and golf tournaments, and be sure you receive their newsletters and event invitations. Some of these are quite affordable or even free.

Get on the A-list for invitation-only parties celebrating the openings of new top brokerage firms, record labels, the premiere issue of a magazine, or movie openings...everybody knows somebody who knows somebody who's willing to get you a ticket.

This may sound strange, and it's not for everyone, but...on any given night of the week Alcoholics Anonymous and their many offshoots hold scheduled meetings – some of which are in the most expensive neighborhoods in town. You don't necessarily have to be an alcoholic to attend: they also sponsor Al-Anon, for people who are close to alcoholics or addicts. For decades people have been joking about AA being the biggest dating service in the country, so if you can find the meetings that attract the wealthy, you're not doing anything so different from anyone else. (*Caveat*: By doing this, of course, you're choosing former addicts as potential Sugar mates.)

Personal Ads

Since the proliferation of online dating, personal ads have lost some of their luster. For awhile, back in the '80s, ads were all the rage, but no more. It's just as well: newspapers don't screen their ads, so anyone can place one, even someone running an escort or dating service. Also, ads aren't conducive to quick or effective matchmaking, since it's impossible to include enough information

And, by publishing your email address, you'd most certainly be attracting spam and worse, a virus or worm that could destroy your PC; most people send and receive personal ads the old-fashioned way – by snail mail, to a P.O. box.

However, personal ads still have their place, namely, in niche magazines such as *Yachting* or *Inc.* These are excellent places to advertise – discreetly – for a Sugar relationship. Spend an afternoon doing research in a major bookstore that has a big magazine section. For almost any human interest you can dream up, there's a magazine: golfing, wine, gourmet food, antique collecting. Choose those that hold some interest for you; for instance, if you love sailing, get a copy of *Yachting*; if you're a dog lover try *Dog Fancy* or *The Pampered Puppy*. Better yet, specialize even more exclusively with a magazine devoted to a specific breed of dog; these are likely to attract wealthier readers. (You can learn about this subculture by watching dog shows on Animal Planet.) Also read general interest magazines catering to the rich, such as *Town and Country* and *Harpers*.

Caveat: Magazines are expensive, and buying a bunch of them can cost a bundle. Libraries carry some – and don't pass up the ones in your dentist's office!

If you're going to place an ad, choose a magazine most likely to be read by the kind of person you're interested in, and first make sure they actually do run personals. As you look through the magazine, pay attention to the regular advertising, as well as reading some of the articles to get a feel for the lifestyle. These specialized groups are actually subcultures, with their own cultural signposts, lingo, style, and accessories.

Here's where the Internet has it all over print: everyone who reads this magazine can easily see your ad – so it had better be discreet. At the same time, you want to let someone know you're not just looking for a date or a spouse; you're looking for something quite specific. It's a bit of a dilemma.

One solution is to write the ad like any other personal, but with a buzz word or phrase thrown in here and there: *arrangement, mutually beneficial, NSA, exchange, discreet, privacy, age not a factor.* Another option is to keep the ad brief, and wait until your first correspondence to talk openly about what it is you're seeking. Even if you just include your age and say *"Age not a factor"* at the end of the ad, a Sugar Baby or Sugar Daddy's antenna will twitch, and they'll respond.

Once they do, the process becomes pretty much the same as the Internet search. If you don't give out your email address, the correspondence phase shouldn't get too dragged out. Be sure anyone who responds to your ad understands this is about Sugar dating. If they didn't realize it, and aren't familiar with the concept, direct them to the Internet to read about it. Of course, you can explain it; but if they see an entire community and movement connected to Sugar dating, they're more likely to respect it.

As I write this, I'm wondering why anyone would want to go the personal ad route now that we have the Internet. I don't see any benefits to the personals, and a lot of drawbacks, for instance, having to explain Sugar dating to a novice. If for some compelling reason personal ads are your thing, though, then go ahead, but in my opinion you're a lot better off with a service like SeekingArrangement.com.

You may have noticed that most of the strategies in this chapter don't involve a lot of unusual activities: the fact of the matter is, you can meet your Sugar Daddy or Sugar Baby anywhere at any time. At a restaurant, or an outdoor café. In an upscale store or a high-end boutique. Drinking your morning coffee. Sipping an evening cocktail. At a car dealership. On the plane.

Learn to integrate your life with your search, until eventually they become one. Knowing that you might meet your Sugar Dream while doing something as mundane as picking up the dry cleaning will motivate you to look good every time you leave the house. Eventually it'll feel easy and natural. Without undergoing a conscious, grueling process, you'll begin to change.

One day you'll look in the mirror and realize you've evolved into the person you wanted to be. As Kurt Vonnegut once said, *"We are what we pretend to be."*

He meant that, after we play at being someone long enough, we ultimately turn into that someone.

That's what happens to people who play in the Sugar Bowl. They become who they wanted, pretended, and hoped to be. They become Sugar Babies and Sugar Daddies. Sweet.

M.B.A.* INTERVIEWING CANDIDATES FOR POSSIBLE M.B.A.**

(*MASTERS IN BUSINESS ADMINISTRATION)   (**MUTUALLY BENEFICIAL ARRANGEMENT)

CHAPTER NINE:

THE SUGAR FAMILY TREE
(*HOMO SAPIEN SACCHAROSE*)

Welcome to the Sugar Daddy Family Tree!

As with any species, there are many varieties of Sugar Daddies – from ordinary to elite, from wannabe to the real deal. None of the categories identified here are to be taken as rigid and immutable; they tend to overlap, and someone could be a Shopping Daddy today and a Mentor tomorrow – or he might be both at once, half and half, or any combination of any varieties. The purpose of identifying Sugar Daddy divisions and subdivisions is not to stereotype, but to explain and expand upon the characteristics of Sugar Daddies; hopefully this will be useful to Sugar Babies in their search, and to Sugar Daddies trying on different styles of Daddying.

Gentleman / Traditional

The father of the Sugar Daddy family tree is the **Traditional (or Gentleman) Daddy**, an entrepreneur multi-millionaire (or billionaire, or...) with a net worth of ten million and higher. He owns condos, mansions, and corporations all over the world, and he gets from one to the other via his own personal jet. He has a well-honed taste for fine food and wine, and an even more developed taste for fine women. He is the Patriarch of the Sugar Daddy kingdom.

A Gentleman Daddy provides his Sugar Babies with cash, shopping sprees, expensive gifts, exotic travel, unique cultural experiences, career advancement if wanted, and even debt relief. His Sugar Baby sometimes does double duty as a "personal assistant" who organizes and maintains his globe-trekking powerhouse lifestyle – so if you see a Daddy profile that says he's looking for a personal assistant, know that it's probably legit.

> I am seeking a Personal Assistant - with a twist. I want someone who will work for me full-time - NOT a mistress, or a sexual relationship, but one which has a sexual aspect to it. I LOVE being around women who are sexy, flirty, exhibitionistic, funny, intelligent, and I am willing to pay quite well. I want someone who can function as a sexretary, who knows computer programs, and who will dress to the nines in short skirts and heels to liven up my time at work. We are not going to sleep together. You'll be responsible for overseeing the care of my homes, make travel arrangements, take care of my

correspondence, messages, emails, etc., and generally be devoted to caring for and making yourself invaluable to me. International travel for both business and pleasure will be involved. Sometimes you'll work nine to five, sometimes in the evenings, and often just sporadically since I'll be out of town. You will have time off to do what you want. The important thing is that you take care of me, be available when I need you or just want company, and be devoted to my interests. You will receive a monthly salary of $6,000 per month, all travel expenses, a generous allowance for clothing, hair, etc. I am known for giving gifts. If it works out, things will get better on the financial front too. The reason sex is not involved is that I have done this before, and concluded that sex gets in the way of the kind of relationship I want. I don't want any complications, jealousy or monogamy. You can live where you want, but I am willing to discuss providing you a place near me. Your private life will be yours.
I realize from reading what women on this site have written that many ads are not real. Be assured that this one is.

That's a pretty elaborate, well-thought-out profile; it's an unusual one, but it describes the Sugar Daddy who wants an assistant that will be part employee, part Sugar Baby. This Traditional/ Gentleman Daddy is rare.

Generally, Mr. Tradition is the guy we hear the most about; he's the Sugar Daddy we see in movies and in the headlines when his cover blows. He might be a CEO, or he could even be a politician. The Traditional Sugar Daddy "keeps" his woman: he buys her a condo at the beach and bankrolls her lifestyle, in which he plays a key part. Perhaps their agreement is that she keeps one or two nights a week free just for him – whether he chooses to exercise his privilege to see her or not. She knows that if he wants her to accompany him somewhere, whether it's a dinner party or a week in Timbuktu, she'll have to drop everything at a moment's notice – and show up at the air strip looking drop-dead gorgeous.

Sugar Babies with Traditional Sugar Daddies live a divine and privileged existence – lazy days at the pool or the (private) beach, shopping and lunching with friends, attending film premieres and A-list concerts, regular spa visits, week-long nutritional or yoga retreats. She might have a personal chef; depending on where she lives she'll probably have her own driver. In other words, her life is pretty close to the way most of us envision it.

Caveat: While she has plenty of time to pamper herself and can do anything her precious little heart desires, the Sugar Baby to this kind of man must always put his needs before hers: that's the deal. It would be difficult, if not impossible, for her to get involved in anything more consuming than a book discussion group; she can't attend school on a steady basis, or run a business, if she's always jetting off to Spain to see a solar eclipse, or accompanying Daddy to his international trade conference. Granted, plenty of women wouldn't mind this trade-off one little bit – but if you have burning personal ambitions of your own, this arrangement won't work for you. Never fear: there are plenty of perfectly suitable Daddies out there.

Cash and Check Daddies

Cash Daddy is just what his name implies: he provides cold hard cash, leaving it in Sugar Baby's purse, under a pillow, or near the kitchen sink. Sugar Baby is well paid, no questions asked, most likely on a per-visit basis rather than a regular allowance. But Sugar Daddies, like everyone else in the world, have issues around money, and some prefer to discreetly drop the greenery some place where they know you'll find it. They genuinely want to help ease your financial pressures – they just don't want to talk about it. If at some point you need more money, ask and ye shall receive – as long as you don't make a big deal out of it. And don't take any of this personally; don't interpret his discomfort to anything you may have done. His money *shtick* is strictly his baggage; as long as he's generous, which Cash Daddies usually are, you've got nothing to worry about.

A **Check Daddy**, again named descriptively, prefers to write checks for a standard monthly allowance so he can write it off as a business expense. Some Daddies even put their Sugar Babies on the payroll of their companies. (If parts of your brain are suddenly blinking like Christmas tree lights, remembering this or that scandal where some corporate honcho's payroll was weighted with invisible female employees – yep, that's exactly what we're talking about.)

Unless you know your Sugar Daddy well, though, it's best *not* to accept checks. We've heard too many stories about phony Sugar Daddies who give a check to an unsuspecting Sugar Baby and cancel it later on. The only check you should accept is one that's certified. You can change this policy after you've been seeing Sugar Daddy a while and are sure he's going to stick around rather than stick it to you with a rubber check.

Debt Daddy

The **Debt Daddy** pays your bills, reduces or erases your credit card debt, and eases your current financial burden. He'll probably ask you about your expenses some time after you begin seeing him – he'll want to know how much you pay out every month, what you owe on credit cards or school loans, etc. The kind of Daddy who wants to take on your whole messy magilla is typically a financial wizard with a streak of the rescuer in him. He gets a lot of satisfaction by helping out a damsel in financial distress. He'll go over your budget and figure out the best way to consolidate your debts, which to pay off first, or whatever financial wizardry he comes up with to improve your situation. He may even offer to negotiate with creditors on your behalf. While he's doing all this, he'll probably tease you and laugh at your lack of money smarts. Don't be offended – it's just an aspect of his *schtick*, part of what pleases him about taking you under his wing this way.

Again, it's probably not a great idea to let someone you hardly know get into your financial panties. For all you know he could be the leader of an identity theft ring, collecting checking account and credit card numbers for sale or distribution. When he first proposes paying down your debt, thank him politely, but say your budget is actually quite simple, but if he would just cover the phone and utility bills…. Once you've gotten to know and trust him, of course, just dump your papers in his lap and let the re-org begin!

The Debt Daddy is doing you a great service. Instead of just handing you a fish, he's teaching you how to fish. He'll get your finances ship-shape and show you how to keep them that way for the rest of your life. Not only should you welcome this opportunity and follow his advice, but for the duration of your relationship with him, pay attention to every word that falls from his lips that's related to finances. I know one woman who became a Sugar Baby solely in order to learn the secrets of great wealth from successful men; today she could be a Sugar Mama if she wanted to.

While the Debt Daddy's a handy guy to have around, he, like

every other type, will never be as popular with Sugar Babies as the beloved **Shopping Daddy.**

The Shopping Daddy

Food for thought: Remember the fun you used to have dressing up dolls when you were little? Well, most little boys were discouraged or forbidden from playing with dolls. Some of them desperately wanted to – and not just the ones on their way to Castro Street SF. These guys look at a beautiful woman and see the doll they never got to play with. It's obvious why Shopping Daddies are so popular with the Babes.

Remember the scene in *Pretty Woman*, at the clothing boutique, when Richard Gere tells the salesmen it's time for some "major sucking up." Gere uses his sense of entitlement as a wealthy man to give Julia Roberts, his weekend Sugar Baby, something she's never gotten before. He's glad he has the power to make the snobby salespeople treat her the way she's always craved.

The only difference between the Gere character and the stereotypical Shopping Daddy is that the latter usually wants to be more involved in the process. So be prepared, honey, 'cuz Shopping Daddy isn't going to simply let you loose in the mall with a credit card: he's going to go with you, to choose what *he* wants you to try on, and he'll watch you go in and out of the dressing room modeling one outfit after another. He may even make an erotic game out of it. He is also likely to be honest in his appraisals. If your taste in clothing happens to clash, you might have to make a few wardrobe compromises – but that's a small price to pay, don't you think?

One delighted Sugar Baby described her first encounter with a Shopping Daddy she met by chance in the mall:

> He started by helping me pick out eye shadow at a cosmetics store. After a brief conversation about the kinds of clothes I like, we went to one of my favorite stores and he bought me a few hot outfits, complete with shoes and bags to match. I felt like it was Christmas. I asked him why he was doing this, what he got out of it. He said he got more joy out of giving than receiving, and he loved to see a beautiful girl so overjoyed and glowing with excitement.

Sugar Babies who prefer to shop alone or with a girlfriend will be relieved to learn that not *every* Shopping Daddy wants to be this intimately involved.

> My previous SD was a big-time high-roller, so we always met in Vegas or another high-end casino town. He'd usually gamble ten hours a day or more, so he'd fly my girlfriends out with me and we'd shop at Caesar's or the Bellagio. I'd shop all day, then wear one of my sexy new outfits for him when we went out to dinner.

Nice work if you can get it.

Shopping Daddies are a special breed. They take pride in their ability to keep a woman looking like a million, on both a financial and aesthetical level. If you're the kind of girl – *and who isn't?* – who'd enjoy having a Shopping Daddy, you should seek one out, possibly even hinting about it in your profile (bluntly stating a desire for a Shopping Daddy might be off-putting to potential SDs; then again, with honesty as the Sugar credo, you might try and risk it). They themselves don't tend to advertise their shopping propensities, but their profile might say something like, "I have more money than people to spend it on," or "I only have myself to buy things for, and that's not enough."

Sometimes you can't tell from a profile that a guy likes to 'shop till he drops' – so watch for clues when you first get together. If he asks to meet in the Food Court at the mall, don't be insulted – Rejoice! And wear your favorite shopping clothes (the ones that slip on and off with ease).

The Mentor Daddy

Needed: Sugar Daddy Mentor for help with school, bills, and what to do next...got ideas?

• • • • •

Sugar Daddy seeking young lady protégé. Can offer guidance and financial security to the right girl who's missing that in her life.

Most of us have had mentors in our lives who've guided us, in our careers or otherwise. While we don't usually associate being a protégé with our dating lives, it frequently happens organically in conventional as well as in Sugar relationships.

Ike Turner started treating Tina badly soon after they became romantically involved, but that doesn't cancel out his professional mentorship of her. She was blessed with that distinct and sexy voice – Ike can't take credit for that – but he nurtured all other aspects of her career. Anna Mae Bullock (Tina's real name) was a hick kid out of some southern backwater when he hired her to sing with his urban blues band and eventually taught her how to be a performer.

Would Anais Nin have written unique and enduring erotica if she hadn't had, as a writing mentor, Henry Miller (as well as his wife June, the sexy Sugar Mama of the threesome)? Would Virginia Woolf have written brilliant novels without her husband Leonard and his printing press? We'll never know for sure, but these mentors were also these women's lovers.

Every day of the week American girls flee the country roads of the heartland and head for New York or another big city, seeking fame, fortune and adventure. She gets some kind of office job, where inevitably one of the older men she works for takes her under his wing. He grooms her for society, showing her where to eat, what to order, which books and magazines to read …. These are mentor relationships.

Sugar Daddies are natural mentors, considering that he is, stereotypically, older than his Baby, and has usually achieved the kind of success most people only dream of. An ambitious Sugar Baby would do well to find a **Mentor Daddy**. Maybe she's a recent graduate trying to figure out what to do with an Art History major; or a woman wanting to quit her dead-end job and start her own business. These protégé Babies are usually single, don't have caring parents to help them, and are precariously navigating life on their own for the first time. For them a Mentor Daddy can be a great source of knowledge, life experience, and wisdom. Sometimes she needs his financial help to get her vision off the ground, but more important, she needs his expertise.

While a Mentor Daddy appears very different, on the surface, from a Shopping Daddy, they actually share a few similarities. Both enjoy molding and shaping a girl to suit their taste. A classic example in literature is *Pygmalion*, better known to modern audiences in its reincarnation as *My Fair Lady*. Eliza Doolittle, as furious as she gets at Professor Higgins, cannot help but fall in love with this man who transforms her from a scruffy flower vendor into a woman who can pass for royalty. He too, oblivious and detached as he is, finds himself in love with the street urchin he tenderly molds into an elegant, articulate lady.

A mentoring relationship can be deeply erotic, layered with elements of power and gratitude. Of all May/December relationships, however, a mentorship is the one least likely to last: Sugar Baby eventually outgrows Daddy, and even rebels against his teachings as a form of manipulation. Their break-up is likely to be stormy and painful, as it unearths buried psychological issues for her. Only later in life, with the perspective age can bring, will she realize how much he meant to her.

Event Daddy / Travel Daddy

> CEO seeks young beautiful woman to accompany me to conferences, meetings, black-tie dinners. Everything first class, all expenses paid.

Travel Daddy ads like this one are self-explanatory. Some **Event Daddies** don't travel that much, but want Sugar Babies to serve as their date at mandatory high-profile business or community events. This type of Sugar Daddy may or may not be married; if he is, his wife either can't or won't accompany him. He may or may not want sex with his Sugar Baby; if not, he'll book them separate hotel accommodations.

All he wants her to be is a delectable piece of arm candy with a reasonable ability to converse and remain poised in social situations. Some Travel and Event Daddies are gay; Sugar Baby acts as his cover, what's known as a "beard," fostering the illusion that he's happily heterosexual.

Event Daddies usually provide a limo, and pay for the designer gowns or anything else they want her to wear. But the more significant perk Sugar Baby gets from a Travel or Event Daddy is access to people she might not otherwise meet, and to a world she'd have a harder time getting into on her own.

Slacker Daddies

> Looking for Sugar Baby for fun times, NSA, no pressure or expectations. Homebody, willing to change if the right girl helps me spend my money creatively.

No, this is not a contradiction in terms; and yes, I know that Sugar Babies come to SeekingArrangement to escape the grubby slacker universe – but when the word is coupled with Daddy, it takes on a whole new meaning. For a certain type of Sugar Baby, a **Slacker Daddy** is perfect, providing a honey-like mellow feeling, rather than the speedy rush of Sugar.

Not every woman *wants* to fly all over the world, wear stockings and high heels every night, and pay scrupulous attention to the condition of her toenails. I'm sure a lot of Sugar Babies can identify with the type of girl who isn't a jet setter, and finds it a strain to have to be 'on' for 24/7. Her idea of a good time is ordering in Chinese and eating it in her pajamas while watching reality TV. She wants a life of leisure without having to sacrifice square footage, designer bags, or car insurance. Her profile might look something like this:

> Laid back girl seeking laid back guy who can afford tickets to movies, rock concerts, ball games, and other sporting events. I want beautiful surroundings and good times without all the headaches and hustle.

Unlike Sugar Babies drawn by the allure of power, ambition, and influence, this Sugar Babe is down-to-earth. The kind of Sugar Daddy she needs isn't that hard to find once you admit you'd enjoy him: most of the time he's *chillaxin'*, as he puts it, by the pool, or killing his buddies in the best play station fight of their lives. While he can provide the fun and relaxation that comes with financial security without having to work for it, his package doesn't include Donald Trump-style thrills and chills. He doesn't know Merlot from Cabernet, and washes down his burgers with a glass of beer.

A Slacker Sugar Daddy may never have lifted a finger in the name of labor. Some have trust funds they've lived on since their 18th birthday. Some are family business heirs, whose checks magically appear in their mailboxes every month. Others are 29-year-old technical geniuses whose brilliant dot-coms or high-end software sold for millions.

This breed of Daddy seeks leisurely adventures such as jet skiing, skydiving, snowboarding, surfing, and the occasional bungee jump. He's likely to schedule these adventures at the last minute; he doesn't have work obligations to make his plans around, or employees relying on him. He wants a Sugar Baby who enjoys the same kind of fun, and who'll be ready to strap on a helmet and join him whenever the mood strikes. He also wants her to come up with new ideas for their adventures. When he's home chillaxin', he likes having her around as company. Otherwise, that's about all he expects from her.

He'll give her a whole wing of the house to come and go as she pleases, and keep his noisy play station and computer equipment on his side of the place. Slacker Dads are casually free and generous with their money, and will hand over a wad of bills without putting her through any drama for it. He'll buy her whatever she wants, pay for their adventures, and give her cash whenever the mood strikes him.

The Slacker Daddy lives comfortably and can afford the finer things in life, but all he really wants is to throw up his feet, put on his headphones and listen to music, or tinker with his electronic toys, and every few weeks or so have an adventure. There's someone for everyone in this world, and I know there are Sugar Babies out there who'd enjoy what a Slacker Daddy has to offer.

Just as there are countless kinds of people in the world, there are more kinds of Sugar Daddies than can fit on our Family Tree. **Retired Daddies** are usually divorced or widowed, and want a Sugar Baby to stand in for the long-gone wife on cruises and RV camping trips. Then there are **Sugar Mamas**, some similar to Sugar Daddies but some very different; we'll talk about them later in this chapter. For now we turn to the Sugar Daddy who could probably fill a whole book himself: The **Married Sugar Daddy**.

Facts

- One in five adults in monogamous relationships, or 22 percent, have cheated on their current partner.
- Nearly 50% of people admit to being unfaithful at some point in their lives, according to the MSNBC.com/iVillage Lust, Love & Loyalty Survey (April 2007).
- According to the same survey, married people with kids – including women with very young children – are nearly as likely to commit adultery as childless couples.
- Half of all marriages end in divorce.

We asked married members on SeekingArrangement.com why they're looking for an extramarital affair. Here are some of their answers:

> I'm in a loveless marriage and I stay only for my children. I'm looking to fill the void in my life.
>
> • • • • •
>
> I'm in an open relationship with my spouse – she knows about and approves of my activity.
>
> • • • • •
>
> I've never been able to be monogamous – I need the excitement of an affair.
>
> • • • • •
>
> I stopped wanting sex with my wife a long time ago – so did she. We're best friends...and there are the kids...I know she knows I cheat, but she pretends not to.

Some men claim that an affair actually helps them stay in their marriage. That does make some kind of sense – when you're hungry you seek food, and when your hunger's been satisfied, you're content with the status quo. One Sugar Baby noted:

> In an SD/SB relationship we honor the marriage to the degree that we're not interested in stealing the man away, just in keeping his fantasies, desires, sexual needs or anything else satisfied—so he can stay in the marriage.

Whatever the reasons for extra-marital affairs, we at SeekingArrangement do not advocate cheating. Our enthusiasm for the Sugar lifestyle isn't an endorsement of adultery, but only of Sugar relationships between consenting adults. We're not responsible for who uses our services – to blame us for adultery would be like blaming hoteliers who let their rooms. The decision to seek a relationship outside of one's marriage is a personal choice and a private matter.

As a society we have huge conflicts about monogamy, marriage, and adultery. Most people give lip service to fidelity, but then turn around and have affairs. Anyone who's thought about the issue with any degree of seriousness recognizes that it's the marital structure that puts both men and women in a bind. Monogamy doesn't come naturally or easily to most human beings – which doesn't mean they shouldn't try to practice it; it just means they frequently fail.

Like the rest of the population, Sugar Babies are all over the map in their feelings and opinions on this issue. Some feel guilty about the wives; some resent not having enough time with their Sugar Daddies; some actually prefer married men for a number of reasons. Here's what they have to say about it:

> I had a married sugar daddy for about a year and it was rather awkward. I always felt a bit guilty when I saw the wedding ring on his finger ... needless to say married sugar daddies are no longer for me.
>
> • • • • •
>
> With married men you can feel like you're stealing from the wife. I went through that for quite some time and expressed it to my married SD. I felt she or the marriage didn't deserve to be treated as he was doing, and that if he was unhappy, she should know so they could do something (or not)... but now I don't really dwell on it anymore. It's his life.
>
> • • • • •
>
> One good thing about the married man is that I don't have to worry about his taxes or house payment or anything else that he might do. When you get involved with a single guy, especially one who's been married and has kids, you have to deal with his past, his obligations to his family, whatever. With a married man, you can enjoy your time with him and take him for what he is.

•••••

I had a relationship with a married man for about five years, so I know how to be discreet. I actually prefer a married Sugar Daddy – it seems to me somewhat normal for a man who has a wife and family to want something different just for himself, whereas I'm weary of the single man (especially in his 40's and older) that doesn't want a serious relationship. Many single men (regardless of how they portray themselves) have issues relating to women, and this is why they're alone. They're the ones you see on the dating sites two or three years after you first meet them.

News Flash: Daddies aren't the only people in the Sugar Bowl with rings on their fingers: some Sugar *Babies* are married too. The double standard is very much alive and well: SDs want their Babies all to themselves.

I'd prefer my Sugar Baby unmarried. I've had SB's who were in other relationships, and how that one was going had an impact on ours. She would be moody, or more or less affectionate depending on what was going on with him. Also, an SB in another committed relationship wasn't always available to travel and do things with me.
•••••
I would never see a married Sugar Baby. No exceptions. As for someone in another relationship, I don't think it's fair to keep her from that. But if that relationship affects ours, that would be a problem we'd have to discuss and work out.

One married Sugar Daddy took a humorous view of it:

I'm a married Sugar Daddy searching for a Sugar Baby. I've met some great women here and many of them like the flexibility that a married SD provides. After all – we men can be pretty needy.

When Mommy Joins Daddy

Sometimes a couple advertises in a profile: both Daddy and Mama together seek a Sugar Baby. The prime motivation for these arrangements is almost always threesomes, or perhaps taking turns with each other while the third one watches; there's a strong element here of voyeurism and exhibitionism.

> You fit the exact description my wife gave me of the kind of woman she would consider an added value to our household. And I fit the description of what you are seeking at least as exactly: pampering girls is what I was born to do, and trying new things is my second nature. We seek a subject, not an object. If your gut feeling tells you to, than contact us without further ado and prepare for a grand and moving life! If this works out the way we hope, I would consider it the highest return on capital in investment history.

In most cases a couple offers the same perks as Sugar Baby would get in any SD relationship. This kind of setup can be a lot of fun for the women, if they develop a friendship – but it can also be a mine field. You're walking into an established couple relationship, inheriting all their old habits, including the dysfunctional. Who do you think ends up in the middle?

> I was a mediator for my last couple, the neutral party in their disputes. Every couple has disputes, and I was the person who could "translate" what each was saying to the other. It wasn't bad or strange; however, if the couple has a lot of dysfunction you may find yourself in the middle of a war, and become just another casualty. It can be emotionally draining, which is why I had to end it with them. But during the good times, what I had and what we shared was a decent, committed relationship where we all re-

spected each other.

Sugar Mamas

Baby what you want me to buy
My accountant's waiting on the phone...
Cause I'm a suga ma-ma-mama
I'm your suga mama, suga mama

—Beyonce Knowles, *Sugar Mama*

Sugar isn't just for Daddy any more, gents – and it hasn't been for a long time. Mama wants some sugar too, and Mama's getting it for herself.

It's common knowledge that women reach their sexual peak some time in their mid- to late thirties, while men are on their way downhill by the time they finish adolescence. Actually, that's an over-hyped "fact"; the only thing that peaks for teenage guys is orgasm: they come fast. Many men learn, as they grow up, how to become better lovers, especially if they have the right women as teachers...but this is beside the point. Women want to be Sugar Mamas for the same reasons that men want to be Sugar Daddies; it's just that historically they haven't had the resources to satisfy their sugar cravings. Still, lust will always find a way: historically, many a horny housewife has commandeered the painter or gardener or pool boy into a part-time Sugar Baby, padding his bills and paying them from the household checkbook.

In conjunction with women's growing economic power and independence has come an increase in the Sugar Mama phenom. There was a time when a woman wouldn't be caught dead paying for sex services – it bears a certain stigma – but that too is changing. A few years ago, Heidi Fleiss, the infamous Mayflower Madam of DC, announced she was going to open a Stud Farm *for women* in Nevada, where prostitution is legal and brothels exclusively for men dot the landscape. Fleiss's plans have yet to materialize, but just the fact that someone's considering such a business is evidence of a sea change.

A lot of men don't seem to understand why a woman would pay for sex: they think women can 'get it for free.' They don't realize that there are appealing aspects of sex-for-pay, primarily, being catered to, with no pressure to perform or reciprocate. Having an ongoing Sugar Baby is different from a night with a male prostitute, but they do have a few elements in common. First and foremost is No Strings Attached sex: that's what the majority of Sugar Mama/Baby relationships are ultimately about. Most Sugar Mamas aren't interested in long dinners, long talks, or long evenings out – they just want to roll around on their Egyptian cotton 200-thread designer sheets with a designer guy who's young, hot, and buff. No complications.

As with Mentoring Daddies, influence and mentorship are often part of the package. Sugar Mamas help groom their Babies for the future by buying and/or choosing their wardrobes, teaching them certain attitudes and skills, and using their influence and network of connections to help them get ahead.

> I am seeking a protégée – male, female, or transsexual – who's interested in an NSA relationship. You must be talented, intelligent, ambitious, and highly sexual. I can offer you financial assistance as well as advice for your future. I am fiery and fun, I have seen much of this world and will be an invaluable friend and lover to you. I hope to change your life for the better.

Just as there are some Sugar Daddies who only want companionship and not sex from a Sugar Baby, so too are there platonic Sugar Mamas. A woman who travels for work might want a Sugar Baby to accompany her on the road as a companion, personal assistant, and protector all rolled into one. Some high-powered Sugar Mamas want a Sugar Baby to take care of the house and animals, to be there when she gets home, and accompany her to events. In most cases, Sugar Baby can do whatever he likes – lounge around all day, play with his friends, go to school – as long as he's available to her at the drop of a hat.

Professional escorts called Walkers hire themselves out to play the role of a date at high profile events. Usually a gorgeous gay (but sometimes straight) man, he offers her the prestige of being seen with a highly desirable young man. A Walker is sometimes called a *Beard*, a closeted gay Sugar Mama's cover-up lover.

The no-sex Sugar Mama, is at least as rare as no-sex Daddies. The male Sugar Baby is Mama's Boy Toy. He can live in or live out; either way, Sugar Mama makes sure he has a wardrobe in keeping with her lifestyle and a ride that won't embarrass her. Depending on the scope of her wealth, she might also pay for school, electronic and other toys, surfing vacations …whatever it takes to keep Baby happy, as long as he goes with her to the Sundance Film Festival, award shows, and vacations on the Riviera.

Just as the financially modest man can be a Sugar Daddy, a woman doesn't necessarily have to be wealthy to be a Sugar Mama. Some men are more motivated by companionship or sex than by money, so it's even easier for a woman to keep a Sugar Baby without blowing her small retirement fund. Most male Babies aren't quite as demanding, materialistically speaking, as their sisters.

For an adventurous, open-minded woman, a Sugar Baby can be an excellent solution to the many and sundry issues faced by older women regarding relationships. He's a convenient source of free labor for all those "boy jobs" like hanging the storm windows, assembling store-bought furniture, or rotating the tires on the car. Back rubs are also a big item on the agenda. Sugar Mamas who *really* don't have money can still keep a Sugar Baby happy with free room and board, all the sex he can handle, and as many extras as she can afford to charge to her credit cards.

Some Sugar Mamas don't want a young, hot, buff man; they want a young, hot, buff woman. In fact, in some parts of the country – San Francisco, New York, Northampton, MA – lesbian sugar arrangements are probably more common than straight ones. Take, for example, this offer:

> A few years ago I inherited my father's estate which includes several assets, all managed under a holding company that I run. Things run fairly smoothly so I have lots of time for play, and I'm looking for a girl to be my business assistant and lover. You will be paid a generous salary with medical and other benefits as an employee of my company, and you will also be given a cash allowance and an apartment as my lover; however, most times you will stay with me in my home.

For women, NSA sex is intensely liberating: it frees them from the constraints of sex-as-love. When both parties are women, well, watch out, because here comes the revolution!

> Being a Sugar Mama is empowering. I took care of the female in my alternative relationship and I felt happy when she was happy, or good when she looked good in the clothes I bought her.

Sugar Mamas *understand* Sugar Babies. They know in their bones the why's and wherefores of a young woman in this kind of relationship – they've been there. Maybe they weren't financially strapped, but almost every woman goes through certain rites of passage regarding career and relationship issues in their 20's. Thus, a lesbian Sugar Baby and Mama sometimes end up as long-term best friends.

> I am a very stable, gentle and generous lady who likes to spend her free time with a female Sugar Baby. I hope to find a female companion for traveling, shopping, dining, theater, spa days, and private fun.

You go, girl!

Sugar Babies On The Family Tree

The queen of the Sugar Baby Family Tree is the **First Daughter Full-Time Sugar Baby**. At the top of the Sugar chain, these Babes expect a monthly allowance and will even put it in writing, so be prepared to sign on the dotted line. Expect to spend $5,000 to $20,000 a month if you want a First Daughter at the pinnacle of her career (like athletes, Sugar Babies rise, peak and lose their stuff in the space of two decades. Read Michael Lewis's book *Money Ball* on adjusting pay scales accordingly). First Daughter Sugar Babies are *kept* women in the traditional sense, with their own condo, high-end car, designer clothes, lifelong spa membership, and a collection of credit cards *you* pay off every month.

These gals – and sometimes guys – are the Major Leaguers. Some of them make sure they have more than one benefactor, keeping Secondary Sugar Daddies on the back burner in case the first one goes sour.

> *You will start off standing*
> *proud to steal her anything she sees*
> *but you will wind up peeking*
> *thru a keyhole down upon your knees.*
> –*Love Minus Zero/No Limit,* Bob Dylan

On their first few dates, Sugar Daddy takes her to fine restaurants for stratospherically expensive dinners; within a month he's helping pay her mortgage, and eventually he makes regular deposits into her retirement fund. Welcome to the Big Show!

How do these Babies get away with it? You might very well ask.

For starters, a First Daughter better be more than everyday beautiful. We're talking about extraordinary movie-star beauty on the order of Angelina Jolie, Heather Locklear, or Charlize Theron; and even so, at this level arm candy doesn't begin to cut it. For what he's shelling out, Sugar Daddy expects intelligence and wit, a woman who can hold her own in sophisticated company. She treats being a Sugar Baby like a job, and spends time honing her skills – by reading the Business Section of a major newspaper to learn financial jargon, and a variety of high-end lifestyle magazines so she can keep Sugar Daddy and herself hip to the latest trends. She cuts out articles on exotic travel destinations, keeps restaurant reviews on file, and monitors changes in men's fashion. She's the engine that runs their high-powered lives.

First Daughter Sugar Baby is poised and composed under all circumstances. She's rarely able to stop being *on*, except perhaps at home alone or with Sugar Daddy. Even then, she'd sooner die than sit around in hair curlers and a bathrobe. The dozens of beauty regimens she undergoes are her own private business, sequestered from Sugar Daddy's awareness; he's not even certain of her real hair color. A Sugar Baby I once knew managed, for three cohabiting years, to keep Sugar Daddy from finding out she had an upper dental plate. (He never mentioned it, so she thinks her ruse worked, but I wonder: Didn't he feel it when they tongue-kissed? Maybe his silence was just politesse. Daddies can be so chivalrous.)

Being a **First Daughter Full-Time Sugar Baby** is a rigorous vocation, but it's as materially rewarding as being a corporate CEO. The money is about the same if not more, and you don't even have to go to the office! But, again, this is no easy gig: only you know if you have it in you to maintain the high standards required of a First Daughter Full-Time Sugar Baby.

The Second and Third Daughters of the Sugar Baby hierarchy are **Student Babies** and **Career Babies**, respectively, and are the most common Baby types in the Sugar universe.

The typical **Student Baby** is working two part-time jobs and taking a full schedule of courses. She's exhausted, and would love to drop at least one of the jobs, but would need help with her tuition. Says one 22-year old Veterinary Assistant from Los Angeles:

> I don't like to be materialistic, but it would totally help out if I got like enough money for a good car and could work less and take more classes. I'd finish so much sooner that way.

The typical **Career Baby** is a recent graduate trying to jump-start her career. She wants access to contacts and information: she wants a mentor. If she's a corporate type she'll most likely look for a CEO Daddy; if she's a musician she'll try to find someone in record production. She knows the fastest way up is through networking, and she wants someone who can open doors, give her advice, and possibly teach her a thing or two about her chosen field.

Student and Career Babies represent a high percentage of SBs, and are far easier to please than the Major Leaguers mentioned above. They'll negotiate for fairly straightforward arrangements, for the typical benefits from a Sugar Daddy that we've discussed throughout this book. Whether a Sugar Daddy opts for one of them or goes for the top of the line depends on what kind of arrangement he wants and what kind of person he prefers to be around: a First Daughter Sugar Baby is a very different kind of woman than a Student or Career Baby, in ways that are self-evident and require no explanation. Needless to say, his choice also depends on his budget: what he spends a month on a Student Baby wouldn't even cover First Daughter's fingernail upkeep!

The **Curious Sugar Baby,** as her name implies, wants to find out about the Sugar lifestyle. She's lured by the luxury and adventure. She might drift in and out of the Sugar community, having a Daddy for six months or a year, then entering a conventional relationship for awhile and returning for more Sugar after that runs its course. Even once she's well acquainted with the taste of Sugar, she remains curious to experience different aspects of it: this Babe's mantra is, and always will be, *Betterharderfastermore!*

Shopping Baby must absolutely have a Shopping Daddy – or, at the very least, a generous one. She's addicted to her Gucci, Dior, or Louis Vuitton, and only a Sugar Daddy can fund her habit – which sometimes gets out of control. When that happens, Shopping Baby gracefully accepts a scolding, or even punishment, from Sugar Daddy. Shopping is a kind of neurosis with this gal: she fully enjoys the cycles of spend, spend, get in trouble, get punished, exercise control – only to eventually start all over again with spend, spend, spend. Addiction counselors call her a shopaholic and treat it as a disease along the same lines as alcoholism. In the HBO series *Big Love,* the character of Nikki is a Shopaholic in a Mormon world; in Sugar lingo she's a classic Shopping Baby.

The **Secretary Sugar Baby** is still alive and well, despite laws against sexual harassment in the work place. There is something very seductive about the boss/secretary dynamic, especially in its earlier incarnation, pre-computer: back then no man would deign to work on the female-identified typewriter. As I've pointed out, power is a huge aphrodisiac, and power is what the boss/secretary relationship is all about.

Many Secretary Sugar Baby/Daddy relationships evolved as an outgrowth of being in close proximity to one another, day in and day out, in highly eroticized work roles. I used to know a Secretary Baby who was a personal assistant to the CEO of a major Fortune 100 company; her job responsibilities were basically to attend to every one of her boss's needs, from fetching his morning coffee to buying presents for his wife – in addition to running his office. She was paid a handsome high six-figure income, and Sugar Daddy bestowed perks on her that the company knew nothing about – or else looked the other way. Ah, the good old days, when men were men and women were secretaries; when harassment was flirting and corruption kept behind closed doors!

The Secretary Baby doesn't just get material benefits; she's also likely to be getting rip-roarin' clandestine sex on the desk or in the darkened conference room high above the lit-up night-time city. Some Boss/Secretary relationships last a lifetime: President Franklin Delano Roosevelt and his 'girl' are a case in point. (Happily, Eleanor had her own female Sugar Baby, as was discovered long after they were all dead and gone.)

Mommies and Daddies For Real

Not everyone comes into the Sugar Bowl free and unfettered, that is, without a past; sometimes the past is a tangible part of the present. I'm talking about kids: a good percentage of Sugar Babies and Daddies are, in real life, mothers and fathers for real. Some of their children are grown and gone, and know nothing of their parent's indulgence in the sweeter side of life. Even younger children are frequently clueless: their parents make sure of that.

> I have children. Not a man in the world has to worry about meeting them; I do not think that it's even part of the deal. My Sugar Daddy is a SEPARATE part of my life, and it suits me fine to keep it that way.

This Sugar Baby's attitude is representative of most. For women, single mothers no less, the Sugar life is something they want to keep as theirs and theirs alone, a little piece of pleasure removed from her kids, her household, and her outsized responsibilities. Her situation is similar to that of the married Sugar Daddy, whose Sugar Baby is a haven from the pressures in his life.

I'm not sure about this, but I have a hunch that keeping the kids separate from Sugar lovers is more of a modern development, that in the past, Sugar Daddies got more involved with their Baby's babies. One woman, now a Sugar Baby herself, fondly recalls her mother's Sugar Daddy.

> My mom had a several-year relationship with an older rich businessman. They'd go out to dinner, dancing, to clubs; they'd take short trips – but mostly it was dinner at our house followed by TV and necking on the couch. I remember lots of jokes and laughter. Sometimes they would just have highballs and play records. I think his

life was so stressful at home with his high-maintenance wife that he liked coming over to our place to relax. No pressure. He didn't have any children of his own, so my kid brother and I were part of the package – he had a family life with all of us. We loved the presents.

Can't you just see them, with their highballs, dancing to Frank Sinatra on the Victrola, with the kids watching and giggling from the top of the stairs? By contrast, here's what a modern-day Sugar Daddy has to say on the subject.

Kids would complicate the relationship for me, and make it difficult to find what I need and am looking for. I understand the demands kids make on a Sugar Baby's life and I believe they should come first when there's a conflict – but I don't want or need any involvement with them. Adding kids into the equation would introduce stress that would not be beneficial to me or the Sugar Baby.

I'm not saying either attitude is better than the other, but merely looking at the way attitudes change over time; my guess is that the latter Sugar Daddy is probably more typical today than the one from a previous generation.

That pretty much covers the Sugar Family Tree, with the notable exceptions of Gay Sugar Daddies. We'll talk about them in the next chapter, along with celebrity Daddies and age differences between Sugar lovers.

"Diamonds are a girl's best friend."

CHAPTER TEN:

A FEW MISCELLANEOUS SWEETS

Celebrity Sugar Daddies

We all know about them: standing in line in the supermarket we read the tabloid headlines: *So-and-so Caught in Love Triangle! Bobby Buys Baubles for Backstage Babes, Wife Takes Him to the Cleaners! What City Counselor Rides So-and-So's Pony?* Tasteless and indiscreet, these stories and scandals captivate us against our better judgment.

Many celebrities – movie stars, athletes, musicians, politicians – regularly dip into the Sugar Bowl. Some manage to keep their affairs strictly private, but more frequently their bubbles burst, and everyone gets treated to every juicy detail of their extra-curricular affairs. For some reason, discovery seems to happen most often in the case of politicians – particularly those who are (a) married; (b) known for their conservative "family" values; and (c) fond of persecuting those they deem immoral, like distributors of pornography, or gay people.

This past June the Chelsea VIP Men's Club in Manhattan instituted an annual **George Burns Memorial Sugar Daddy Award**, naming as their first honoree Eliot Spitzer, the former governor of New York who was caught hiring prostitutes and slipping paramours onto the payroll. Personally, I think VIP's choice is misguided. In celebrating a man like Spitzer, who abused his power, publicly humiliated his wife, and screwed the taxpayers of New York, they've compromised the positive spirit of the Gentleman Sugar Daddy – and every other type. I ask you, is Spitzer who we want as the model of a Sugar Daddy? Is his behavior worthy of awards? Spitzer is not a Sugar Daddy; far from being a Sugar Daddy type, he should have received the title "King of Johns" … yes, John, the common term prostitutes refer to their anonymous clients.

VIP was off to a good start when they named the award after George Burns, a lovable old coot who was a category all his own: **Benevolent Daddy**, perhaps. Burns never missed an opportunity to wolf whistle a pretty girl or make eyes at passing women

– but he certainly never humiliated his wife, Gracie Allen, with whom he stayed until she died. (George himself lived to be over a hundred.) I don't know what Georgie had going on the side – and I don't particularly want to know. In everything Burns said and did he honored Gracie – he even wrote a book about her called *Gracie: A Love Story*. If he had Sugar Babies on the side – and I have a feeling he was all hat and no cattle – then he would have treated them fantastically, and never, *never* would have let it damage his marriage.

The VIP Club added insult to injury with their gang of honorable mentions: Woody Allen, Tom Cruise, Jack Nicholson, OJ Simpson, Hugh Hefner, Verne Troyer, Bill Maher, Tommy Lee, and Fred Durst. While these men all have a penchant for dating young girls, this alone does not a Sugar Daddy make. In fact, I'm not sure any of these guys should qualify as SDs – they're just old coots who pounce on the first vulnerable young woman they see. Woody Allen turned his girlfriend's teenage daughter into his Sugar Baby and later his wife. Worse even is the man who may have murdered his wife; in my book, the VIP Club lost all credibility by honoring – *honoring!* – OJ Simpson.

Maybe the Club meant the whole thing as tongue-in-cheek: maybe they're actually dissing Sugar Daddies. Because if these are the sweet guys, heaven deliver us from the sour!

There is one man, and only one, on the list about whom we can all agree, and who I'm one hundred percent sure qualifies as The Real Thing – hell, he almost invented Sugar Daddies and Babies! Can you guess who I'm talking about? He's the Ultimate Sugar Daddy of all time. His name is…

Hugh Hefner : Ultimate Sugar Daddy

While Sugar Daddies existed long before Hugh Hefner came along, he, more than anyone else, perfected the art of Sugar dating – and not just for himself, but for every man in the civilized world. The first issue of *Playboy*, with Marilyn Monroe as the centerfold, sold 50,000 copies, enabling Hef (his nickname since high school) to publish the next issue, and go on to build *Playboy* into an empire, and himself into a living legend. Beautiful girls of all ages flock to his side. With the exception of a minority of rigidly anti-porn crusaders, women respect and appreciate Hef, partly because he's the quintessential gentleman, but, more important, because he pioneered the cause of equal sex rights for women, and this was way before anyone else even dared to think about it. "*Playboy*," he once said, "was founded on the notion that nice girls like sex too."

Like the rest of the economy, *Playboy* is falling on hard times. It's a sad state of affairs when an iconic 83-year-old multimillionaire has to lay off staff or go bankrupt – yet that may be what's happening. Mixed in with the gossip, speculation, and half-truths about failing banks, collapsing markets and dried-up credit, were rumors that Hef's happy household was splitting up, that his three twenty-something blonde Sugar Babies were moving out of his Los Angeles mansion for budgetary considerations. As far as we know, he and Holly have split up, but there are new girls in the wings, ready to become Hugh's new Sugar Babies.

From its inception, *Playboy* was revolutionary. It was the first mainstream publication to print pictures of naked women right next to intelligent and trenchant articles of social commentary. A widely popular joke, still told today, was, "I read it for the articles."

Every issue featured probing stories about prominent thinkers, celebrities, movers and shakers. In the pages of *Playboy*, President Jimmy Carter confessed to having "lusted in my heart." John Lennon and Yoko Ono revealed things about themselves told nowhere else, and the interview was later published as a book. Interviews with everyone from rock stars to world leaders ran for twenty, thirty or more pages. The best contemporary writers vied to get into *Playboy*: Philip Roth, Joyce Carol Oates, Kurt Vonnegut. But more than this, *Playboy*'s chief purpose was to serve as an instruction manual for men who aspired to be, like its creator, a carefree playboy.

In what are now called "lifestyle" articles, the magazine shaped a universe with Hefner's taste indelibly stamped on everything in it. Pictorials of swanky homes exhibited up-to-the-minute decorating trends, including Hef's famous, well-stocked round bed. Men's clothing, electronic equipment, cars, restaurants...*Playboy* gave American men a crash course in sophistication. They soon believed that if they furnished their living room with a leopard skin sofa and reclined on it in a smoking jacket, they might turn into a clone of their idol.

Hugh Hefner called himself a Playboy, not a Sugar Daddy, but in his case (not in every case, mind you!) they're one and the same. Unlike most producers of adult material, Hef is highly esteemed by the publishing industry – and, as one website points out, he's managed to pull it off while still in his pajamas! Girls still want to be with him, and guys still want to be him.

Hefner donates to anti-censorship groups, sex research institutions, and various kinds of film organizations. He also gives generously to the Democrats. When Sarah Palin emerged from the snows of Alaska into the bright light of public scrutiny, Hef's assessment was that she'd make a terrific *Playboy* centerfold. "Imagine what she's like when those glasses come off," he said. "It would be a new definition of the word *vice* in vice-president." Only Hugh Hefner could get away with saying something like that.

Hugh Hefner trivia:

- A species of rabbit is named in his honor (*Sylvilagus palustris hefneri*).
- He's the first magazine publisher to become a major celebrity.
- He had a Genius IQ of 152 in high school but was an "unenthusiastic" student.
- He was arrested in 1963 for possessing "indecent" photos of actress Jayne Mansfield.

No matter how the current economic situation shakes down, Hugh Hefner will always be the world's Ultimate Sugar Daddy.

Marilyn Monroe: Sugar Babe Extraordinaire

Some Sugar Babies are born, not made. If America held a Miss Sugar Baby Pageant, the winner would surely be Norma Jean Baker, aka **Marilyn Monroe**. Marilyn wasn't a Sugar Baby in the traditional sense: she did not intentionally set out to find a Sugar Daddy, having her own ambitions of super stardom. Never the less, she became a Sugar Baby by default, in her life and on the screen. She attracted wealthy and accomplished men – Yankee Clipper Joe DiMaggio, playwright Arthur Miller, and even President John F. Kennedy, to name just a few – who showered her with expensive gifts and outsized attention. Up until his own death a few years ago, DiMaggio had flowers delivered to her grave every day of his life.

On the screen, Marilyn was typecast as a Sugar Baby early on. In *How to Marry A Millionaire* she declared, "I'd rather marry a rich man than a poor man," the woman perhaps speaking through the character. The distinction blurred, at least to her audience. Only after her death did the world learn anything of the real Marilyn – that she was no ditzy blonde, but fairly intelligent; that she was a dedicated actor, but her extraordinary physicality overshadowed her work, which was never taken seriously. Men, of course, adored and wanted her. Women either hated her out of envy, or wanted to be her – or both. Her legions of fans never knew how hurt and frustrated she was about being seen only as a sex symbol.

> *Even when you died*
> *Oh the press still hounded you*
> *All the papers had to say*
> *Was that Marilyn was found in the nude...*
> —Elton John, *Candle in the Wind*

Gentlemen Prefer Blondes, the archetypal Monroe flick, could be taken for a Sugar Baby manifesto. Marilyn plays Lorelei, a showgirl on tour with her stage partner Jane Russell. Lorelei is engaged to a pipsqueak oil man (yesteryear's version of the techie geek), and Russell, a knockout in her own right, is charged with keeping Lorelei out of man trouble – which, predictably, fails. Pipsqueak's father thinks Lorelei is a cruel mercenary exploiting his son, and tries to get rid of her. In their climactic confrontation, Lorelei/Marilyn speaks with pride and self-confidence for all Sugar Babies when she says that wanting money and jewelry doesn't make her cruel or heartless – she actually does love Pipsqueak. She claims the right to use her looks for material gain since, she points out, men use their money to impress girls. Why shouldn't a pretty girl use her assets?

The movie's highlight is the song-and-dance number *Diamonds Are a Girl's Best Friend*.

> *Girls grow old, and men grow cold*
> *and we all lose our charms in the end.*
> *But square-cut or pear-shaped*
> *these rocks don't lose their shape.*
> *Diamonds are a girl's best friend.*

(I hereby nominate this as the official Sugar Baby national anthem. You can see and hear Marilyn sing it at: http://www.lyrics.com/index.php/artists/lyric/marilyn-monroe-p-7158-lyrics-diamonds-are-a-girls-best-friend-t-9931106. You'll never be the same, believe me!)

Marilyn was the centerfold in the very first issue of *Playboy* magazine, which came out in 1953. Hugh Hefner owns the burial vault next to hers at Westwood Memorial Park in Los Angeles. It's only fitting that the quintessential Sugar Baby and the ultimate Sugar Daddy will spend eternity side by side.

May/December, Jailbait, Ripe Fruit: What's In a Number?

Some people say *age ain't nuthin' but a number* – but deep in our hearts we all know that's a crock. Sure, some octogenarians are young at heart, while a lot of twenty-somethings burn out early – but for most people the aging process follows a similar arc that affects us in predictable ways. As we grow older we constantly change – in our outlook, appearance, behavior, and desires – and it cannot help but affect our relationships. When two people with a wide age disparity get together, the gap in years and experience make for a geometrical increase in the number of things that can go wrong – or right.

Age plays a key part in Sugar arrangements, since the parties involved tend to be far apart in years. In the past, the stereotypical Sugar Baby was in her early twenties, while most Sugar Daddies were over sixty. Although that's still common enough, age configurations today are all over the map.

A substantial number of Sugar Daddies on SeekingArrangement. com are surprisingly young; elsewhere we discussed the reasons that more men make their fortunes at a younger age than in previous generations. Even more surprising, many of today's Sugar Babies are in their forties and fifties – and they don't lack for suitors. Some Sugar Daddies even prefer them.

> As we get older our desire for something stable and long-term seems to increase. You'd be surprised how many young women cannot understand this. That's exactly the reason I changed my profile to request that only women over 40 contact me.

These days, popular slogans tell us "Forty is the new thirty," or "Sixty is the new fifty," meaning that we're looking and feeling much younger than people did in the past at the same chronological age. Because science has learned so much about nutrition, exercise, the brain's functioning, and health care, most of us look and feel nothing like our grandparents did at our age – or even like our parents. We expect to keep doing the things we enjoy all our lives, and that includes an active sex life. One collection of older women's erotica goes by the title *Ripe Fruit*.

Thus, an older man isn't necessarily looking for a sweet young thing anymore. He wants more than a pretty face; he wants someone he can talk to. Additionally, there've always been younger men who lust after older women, and vice versa. Think Mrs. Robinson in *The Graduate*.

There's a dangerous aspect to the matter of age differences. Call it *Jailbait:* just stay clear of underage Sugar Babies, whether you're a Sugar Daddy *or* a Mama. It's illegal to have sex with someone under the age of consent (which varies from state to state), and in recent years the penalties for doing so have increased. Genuine concern about child molestation has gone out of control, creating an atmosphere of generalized hysteria. A vigilante mentality is directed at teenagers who have sex, on the premise that if an older boy (18 and up, usually) has sex with an underage girl – even one who's less than a year younger than him – is a sex crime. If you've ever watched the NBC reality series *To Catch a Predator* you know what I mean. (Today, even having an online conversation with an underage person may be a felony offense, especially if the conversation involved sex.)

Take the case of Generlaw Wilson, a 17-year-old Georgia man arrested for having consensual oral sex with his 15-year-old girlfriend. Wilson was sentenced under a child molestation law, even though the girl did not bring charges, and asked the court to drop the case. The District Attorney offered Wilson a reduced sentence if he'd admit to being a sex offender – but he would have had to register as one, and couldn't live at home with his baby sister and the rest of his family. (After serving two years of a ten-year prison sentence,

Wilson was released when the Georgia Supreme Court ruled his sentence cruel and unusual punishment.) Wilson's case isn't all that unusual; hundreds more like it exist. A lot of so-called *sex offenders* on those blacklists are actually guys who simply behaved like teenage boys when they *were* teenage boys, and got branded *Pervert* for the rest of their lives.

The moral of the story: underage Sugar Babies should be avoided like the plague. It can ruin your reputation, your career, and possibly your life.

Once labeled a sex offender, you never get a reprieve. Your name is published on the Internet and circulated to the neighbors. The places you can legally reside are severely limited. This is no joke. When it comes to young people and sex, the country's gone berserk - so if you meet a creature who you suspect is underage, start running and don't stop until you find some old lady to bed down with!

This goes for Sugar Mamas: women don't have paycheck parity yet, but they're just as suspect and punishable as a man if they have intimate contact with a too-young person. Doing day care or teaching school must be paranoid hell these days, with bureaucrats and peers watching like hawks, ready to yell "*Gotcha!*" if a teacher happens to give a student so much as a comforting pat.

Don't forget that young girls lie about their age all the time. SeekingArrangement doesn't require members to provide age verification upon registration, but if a girl, or guy, is obviously too young, his or her picture will not be approved. All reported suspicions are investigated, and the person is removed, blocked from the site, and asked not to return until they're eighteen, so if you do suspect someone of being under age, report them immediately.

Gay Male Arrangements

Gay men are unparalleled connoisseurs of the Sugar Daddy phenomenon. These guys have been playing Daddy games for decades, at least since personal ads became popular, and probably a lot longer. Straight people only know about the ads because they're public; we don't know what went on in private before then.

For gay men, Daddy – as well as Baby – is a powerful erotic symbol. Not that this isn't true for heterosexuals; it's just that gay men tend to be more open to sexual exploration, and have fewer conflicts about role-play. Whereas a woman might not feel comfortable facing, much less admitting, an erotic component to a Sugar Daddy arrangement, gay men embrace this aspect.

Additionally, there's quite a bit of money floating around the gay community. It's a community of men only, and men in our society earn more money than women. Also, until very recently, gay men's money wasn't spent on kids. Do the math.

Between greater economic resources and more liberated sexual attitudes, gay men have more opportunity to explore and refine the complexities of Sugar Daddy-hood. Some gay men take the aging process hard, in a community where youth and beauty are highly prized. Thus, the Daddy role becomes their saving grace. In *The Ugly Duckling*[1]* writer Simon Sheppard depicts one man's transformation from depressed aging queen to studly Sugar Daddy.

> This is hopeless. Nobody wants an ugly old thing like me'...He resolved to go home and bring the whole unhappy night to a close. As he set off toward his lonely apartment, he noticed a young man in the semi-darkness,

1 * The Ugly Duckling by Simon Sheppard. Published in *Happily Ever After*, ed. By Mike Ford and in *Hotter Than Hell and Other Stories* by Simon Sheppard.

all alone, leaning up against the chain-link fence. The young man seemed to be looking in his direction. As he walked by, the man's gaze seemed to follow. Several steps beyond, he stopped and turned. The young man was turned toward him. He was tall and skinny and cute. Swann froze in his tracks....'Hello, Daddy,' the tall, skinny boy said... At first, Swann thought he should feel insulted. But he didn't, in fact, feel insulted. He felt something entirely new.

You don't have to take my word for any of this: pick up some gay porn / erotica and you'll see what I'm talking about. If you're uncomfortable browsing in the porn section of a gay bookstore, you can easily find this stuff online, or at Good Vibrations in San Francisco or Berkeley – or in their catalog. I know of at least one anthology devoted to male-on-male Daddy stories - *Doing It for Daddy* – but almost any gay collection will probably include a daddy story or two.

When gay men arrange a Sugar relationship, it's usually an extension of the sex rather than vice versa. Living as Sugar Daddy and Baby enhances their sex, as their lifestyle feeds into the Daddy/Baby dynamic. While many of the same issues arise as in a heterosexual Sugar arrangement, they tend to be resolved differently. For instance, a male Sugar Baby isn't likely to worry, before a first meeting, that "all he wants from me is sex" – most likely that's what Baby wants too! And negotiations around money are likely to be turned into an erotic game.

And so...let the games begin! In the next chapter we'll talk about specific ways to keep the Sugar sweet and make it even sweeter.

CHAPTER ELEVEN:

KEEP IT SWEET, MAKE IT SWEETER, GO FOR SWEETEST

The terms most often used to define Sugar arrangements are *No Strings Attached* (NSA), *mutually beneficial*, and *negotiated*. The parties tacitly agree to these principles as something to strive for, and hopefully achieve, within their relationship. They are the Sugar Bowl equivalent of marital vows.

By its very nature, the lovers in a Sugar relationship are always looking for new ways to please one another. When you trust that the other person has your best interests at heart, you feel secure and can relax: you don't have to worry about *getting my share*. Admit it – that's what most of us do in our relationships: we watch out for *Numero Uno*. Afraid of being cheated of what we think is our due, we weigh and balance and mentally keep score. Anyone who's been in a more-or less-normal, traditional relationship is familiar with the syndrome.

If, on the other hand, you've ever had the good fortune to love someone in a way that transcends this trivial nonsense, where you didn't obsess about your needs and wants and getting your share, but instead cared so much about the other person that you were more focused on pleasing him or her than yourself...if you've ever been in love *like that*, you know the difference. In traditional relationships we resent the other person if we think they're not giving us enough; resentment alternates with its companion emotion, guilt, any time we think we're not doing enough of the giving. Two sides of the same coin, these emotions are toxic, not just to the relationship, but to one's very soul. And yet and still, we call it *love*.

> *Well I've been where you're hanging*
> *and I think I can see how you're pinned.*
> *When you're not feeling holy*
> *your loneliness says that you've sinned.*
> —Leonard Cohen, *The Sisters of Mercy*

The magical, lovely, and wonderful thing that happens when each person is focused on *giving* rather than *getting* is that you end up getting more than you even knew you wanted. Resentment and guilt rarely show their ugly faces, except perhaps in an occasional disagreement. The relationship is all about pleasure, respect, appreciation, and fun.

When thought of in these terms, a Sugar arrangement can have personal meaning beyond one relationship: it presents opportunities for lessons in giving – a spiritual practice if ever there was one.

> *When we give from the heart, we do so out of a joy that springs forth whenever we willingly enrich another person's life. This kind of giving benefits both the giver and receiver. The receiver enjoys the gift without worrying about the consequences that accompany gifts given out of fear, guilt, shame, or desire for gain. The giver benefits from the enhanced self-esteem that results when we see our efforts contributing to someone's well being.*
> — *Nonviolent Communication*, Marshall Rosenberg

In the well-functioning Sugar arrangement, both parties get what they want: that is a guiding principle. As pointed out repeatedly, this can only occur if everyone is perfectly clear and honest about their expectations, hopes, and desires.

The NSA aspect of an arrangement means that both parties recognize they have no hold over one another, except whatever they've mutually agreed to for a finite period of time, whether that period is predetermined or not. Browse the profiles on a site like SeekingArrangement.com and notice the recurrence of the phrases *no strings, no games, no drama*. These are all ways of saying *we don't own each other*. People aren't pets – you cannot *own* them – and in Sugar arrangements this is taken seriously. Each person's independence remains intact; it's the one thing that's non-negotiable.

Both the Sugar Daddy and Sugar Baby should spend time, thought, and imagination dreaming up ways to give each other pleasure. As they say in the old hippie and New Age subcultures, *practice random acts of kindness and senseless acts of beauty.*

A Sugar Daddy Gives...

...without too many words or details.

...designer shoes at random; red ones never fail.

...the security of knowing you have more than you'll ever need.

...expensive gifts professionally wrapped in shiny paper and curly ribbons.

The idea is to make it appear, and even be, effortless. If you're thinking too hard about what to give, then you're missing the point. Outside of predetermined details, like allowance amount or travel expenses, the majority of your gifting should be spontaneous. You'll be irresistible to her.

A Sugar Baby Gives...

...enthusiasm and the spark of youth.

...HEAT: to look at, walk with, or be next to.

...a reason to go to your high school reunion.

...adventure, change and newness: the keys to eternal youth.

Sugar: The Key to Eternal Youth

Elegant five-course dinner for two: $385.60

Lapis necklace (Gift for SB): $250.00

Her taxicab home: $12.50

Feeling 20 years younger: Priceless

Sugar Daddy might not even realize he's looking for it, but one reason older men or women want younger lovers is that it helps them recapture their own youth. This Sugar Baby gift is a no-brainer: all she has to do is *be*. The mere presence of her young self gets Sugar Daddy feeling younger and livelier. Youth is a gift bestowed on each of us for a brief period of time; unfortunately, we seldom realize how precious it is until after it's gone.

The smart Sugar Baby knows she holds this gift, and she derives great pleasure out of sharing it. When she lets all that youthful energy emerge, she becomes more tuned into it herself. Whereas most of us don't give much thought to being young while we are – hence the saying *Youth is wasted on the young* – we can't help but notice the "sweet bird" when it is reflected back at us by the eyes of an older companion – and the gift comes full circle.

For this reason the savvy Sugar Baby doesn't dampen her youthful impulses in a misguided attempt to appear sophisticated. She allows free rein to her playful creativity, even if she acts a little silly, in a fun kind of way, sometimes.

She almost always has music playing at home, and she dances with Sugar Daddy in the kitchen. Sometimes she'll greet him at the door in a crazy or sexy costume (see Idea #1 in the list further down). Any time she gets a notion to do something unusual and spontaneous – say, go for a ferry ride in the middle of the night – she makes sure they do it then and there (just be certain the ferry in question actually runs all night so you don't get stranded!). Most people lose spontaneity as they age, but when encouraged by a young lover, it all comes back (just like riding a bike). For the older person, getting in touch with youthful feelings, even temporarily, is a real Sugar high.

Caveat 1. If you – or your Sugar Daddy – are one of the musically open-hearted people of the world who enjoy listening to a wide variety of genres, you can skip this section. Such people are few and far between; most of us get stuck in the music that formed the sound track of our transition to adulthood, in our 20's or 30's, and we never listen to anything new again. There's always been a musical disconnect between the generations: the battle begins with one's parents during adolescence, and expands to the wider world later on. The intensity of this feud has shown signs of ebbing ever since music such as that of the Beatles and the Rolling Stones crossed generational lines, but musical intolerance will always be with us. It's as if older ears are too worn out to process new or different musical configurations.

Thus, if Sugar Baby's grooving to Kanye West, while her Sugar Daddy thoroughly despises hip hop, you've got a conflict every time you flip the dials on the car radio or slip a CD into the player. He'll play the Grateful Dead for hours on end, but chances are that unless Baby's a second- or third-generation Deadhead, it'll put her right to sleep. The solution? You could each get under your separate MP3 devices…but who wants to do that?

This is one area where older folks can be horribly inflexible, so I'm afraid it's up to Sugar Baby to cultivate tolerance and consideration: if he really can't stand a musical genre, don't play it around him – you'll just irritate him and not have fun that night. Yes, it is regrettable when lovers can't share music – but it's one of the hazards of dating outside of one's peer group. Maybe you'll stumble into a genre – jazz is frequently a unifier – that you can both agree on; again, odds are better that Sugar Baby will take to one of his old collections. Good luck.

Caveat 2. Some Sugar Daddies are honest-to-god homebodies who really just want to stay home and watch videos, eat popcorn, and mess around on the sofa. These guys work hard and/or have many stress factors in their lives; being with Sugar Baby is the only time they can relax. In this case, needless to say, Sugar Baby shouldn't insist on going out to party all the time. Your Sugar Daddy might not care if he ever has a Sugar high; Sugar Baby should respect that.

More often, however, young people tend to underestimate older ones, by assuming they can't or won't do anything too rigorous, like hiking or bike riding, or dancing the night away. Sometimes a Sugar Baby is afraid her choice of activity might make her look unsophisticated, so she holds herself in check. She needs to realize that if she never shows her bubbly side, and lets him call all the shots, they could get so squashed into that couch it would take an earthquake to unseat them. There's nothing inherently wrong with being a couch potato; great fun can be had with two people and a sofa. But eventually one or both of you are bound to get bored. If Sugar Baby is proactive, she can avert a Sugar crash by taking control and revitalizing Daddy. Forget all those silly notions about sophistication. Learn to trust yourself.

Trust yourself
And look not for answers where no answers can be found.
Don't trust me to show you love
When my love may be only lust.
If you want somebody you can trust, trust yourself.
—Bob Dylan

What Does Sugar Daddy Appreciate? Let Us Count the Ways

Food for thought:

> Never miss an opportunity to make others happy,
> even if you have to leave them alone in order to do it.

(Author Unknown)

Think about the kinds of things Sugar Daddy likes to eat, to do, to have done to him. In a typical arrangement, he comes to Sugar Baby for R&R; she's a haven from the pressures of his life. While just being your sexy and attentive self is probably plenty for him, everybody likes a surprise once in a while. By giving him one, you'll show that you appreciate him. Below is a list of specific "appreciation-showing" ideas. Try one, some, all, or none of them: only you know what feels natural to you, as well as what your Sugar Daddy might enjoy. While there must be at least 50 Ways to Please Your Lover, for now we'll stick to a more manageable ten.

1. *Cook and Serve Him an Aphrodisiacal Dinner.* This depends somewhat on your abilities and enthusiasms in the kitchen, but if you like to cook and do it passably well, chances are you will make him dinner at some time or other during the course of the relationship. That said, for one dinner trade in the usual pasta concoction for a meal made exclusively of foods known for their aphrodisiacal qualities. Get yourself a copy of Isabel Allende's *Aprhodite: A Memoir of the Senses* for inspiration and recipes. Amazon calls the book *"a long, savory, enthralling ode to sensuality."*

   Most people know the more popular foods that are considered sexy. Oysters top the charts; Allende calls them, *"those seductive tears of the sea, which lend themselves to slipping from mouth to mouth like a prolonged kiss*". More of the ocean's sensual bounty includes shrimp, clams, and mussels. Other foods liable to provide a hormonal charge are asparagus spears, truffles rooted out of the depths of the earth (*muy expensivo!*); and, of course, almost anything chocolate. These are the most well-known aphrodisiacal foods, and they really do work, though different people have differing reactions to them. Make it pretty, delicious, subtle, and light: you don't want to overstuff yourself or him, lest you end up falling asleep, bypassing dinner's potential side effects!

2. *Give Him Gifts.* Who says Baby's the only one here who should get presents? Maybe you can't afford to buy him a Rolex, but you probably can afford a bobblehead of his favorite baseball player, or a whimsical car decoration. Be creative. One Sugar Baby I know came across a list in a men's magazine of "Ten Things Every Single Man Needs," and she used it as the basis for a Christmas package. The only items I still remember are a Frank Sinatra album, smoking jacket, deck of cards, and a blender. She bought a blender *refrigerator magnet* and got the smoking jacket second-hand (it wasn't really for wearing, just part of the fun – but if you're flush you could do this item for real). Her Sugar Daddy was delighted as he unwrapped and laughed over one item after another.

3. *Use Technology Creatively.* Send him text messages – sexy or friendly or loving, depending on your mood. Tease him with pictures of yourself sent via phone, email, or any other gizmo you have with photo capability. You can also put sexy pictures of yourself into your own greeting cards made with

a simple software program like Print Explosion. Give cards at random, not just on holidays.

4. **Wash his hair.** *"I wanna talk to you, I wanna shampoo you, I wanna renew you again and again."* So sang Joni Mitchell in *"All I Really Want,"* an ode to unselfish love. All I really want *you* to do is shampoo his hair…*with your toes!* (Figure it out.)

5. **Forego The Money Once in A While.** If your arrangement is that Sugar Daddy gives you cash or a check on every visit, politely decline once or twice. Let him know you genuinely like spending time with him (but be clear this is a one-time gesture, not new policy!). As you can imagine, this really says something: he'll be floored.

6. **Dress Up for Him.** Dressing Up doesn't *always* have to mean lingerie. Sure, that's part of your repertoire – and don't forget to include corsets; these days the variety is diverse and stunning, and nothing else gives a woman that hourglass figure. Still, even the sexiest or flimsiest ensemble can get old after awhile. (Besides, how long do you really keep the thing on?)

    I'm talking now about **Dress-Up**, the game you played as a kid, turned up a notch with erotic overtones. Greet him at the door in a kooky getup, say, a black raincoat with nothing underneath, a toy gun in your pocket and a big floppy hat on your head. You're a spy, or a 1930's-era gun moll – whatever you, and he, want to pretend, the wackier the better. Or play geisha in a silk kimono from a second-hand shop. If you can get Sugar Daddy to join in the fun (don't push it if he resists), buy him, say, a kid's firefighter hat and tell him to "put out my fire."

7. *Wake Him With A Surprise.* One night when Sugar Daddy's sleeping over, tell him you have to be some place early the next morning. (If you're no good at these kinds of "lies," you won't be able to pull this off, but if you *can*...) Get out of the house before he's even out of bed. It shouldn't take you long to get dressed, since you'll be naked under your buttoned-up coat. Go for a ride and pick up jam and croissants for breakfast; or just sit in the car and read the paper for half an hour. If all goes as planned, he'll still be in bed when you return, throw off the coat, climb in next to him, and warm your chilly body up and down and against his toasty one. (This feels sooooo gooood!)

8. *Read to Him.* Be sure to "lose" the remote control before a tired Sugar Daddy comes in after a hard day's work and collapses on the sofa. Sit down and put his head or his feet in your lap, and open up a book of erotic stories you've hidden between the couch pillows. Or, if you have the inclination, try writing your own erotica (get a copy of Susie Bright's e-book, *How to Read a Dirty Story*). You could even put him and/or you into a story. How long do you think it'll take for his exhaustion to evaporate?

9. *Play Games.* No, not mind games. And no, not Strip Poker either, it's been done to death. Instead, choose your favorite card or board game – Scrabble, Monopoly, UNO, whatever – and whoever wins gets to choose that night's sexual activity or fantasy. You'll need some guiding rules here; for instance, you can't shave his legs if you know it gives him the creeps. By the same token, he can't make you "pull a train" because you lost a game of dominoes.

10. *Indulge His Fantasies*. Make a pact with yourself, not necessarily directly to him but fine if you want to, that you will always indulge Sugar Daddy's sexual fantasies (with the exception of hated, feared, or truly dangerous acts). Encourage him to tell you, if he hasn't already, what those fantasies are. Tell him yours. Naturally, he'll want to reciprocate and indulge *you* some of the time.

If you need help to comfortably articulate sex fantasies, pick up a book at Good Vibrations: *Sex for the Clueless* by Marcy Sheiner, *Exhibitionism for the Shy* by Carol Queen; Annie Sprinkle's *Spectacular Sex*, or a few hundred other choices – when it comes to sex, everyone's got something to say.

One book I particularly recommend, not necessarily for fantasy value, but for general sexual self-knowledge, is *The Erotic Mind* by Jack Morin.

Surprises for Your Sugar

Daddies: Men are always asking *What do women want?* When in truth, most women aren't all that difficult to please – at least not when it comes to gift-giving. So many tangibles make them purr – flowers, jewelry, a pretty card with genuine sentiments on it. Here's a list of ten Surprises for Your Sugar.

1. *Flowers*. Don't yawn – flowers never get old, so bring or send them frequently. For a change of pace, skip the flower shop, instead picking a bouquet from the side of the road. And never pass up a field of tiger lilies without stopping to pick some!

2. *Gift certificate or DIY pedicure.* Buy her a gift certificate for a pedicure, or, better yet, DIY: polish her toenails, massage her feet with good lotions or creams. If you're in the mood, try shaving her legs in the bathtub; I'm told that women find it highly erotic.

3. *Food.* Bring her chocolates, gourmet olives, three fresh oysters...even just a hunk of designer cheese you know she particularly likes. If you have any cooking skills at all, use them. *Caveat:* If Sugar Baby's always on a diet, or worried about her weight, fuggedaboudit. *Dieter's Substitute:* A basket of fancy fruits.

4. *Jewelry.* Diamonds really *are* a girl's best friend but you don't have to buy her diamonds every week, or ever if you can't afford them. Other kinds of precious stones can be had for a more reasonable cost - lapis, for instance, or jade, are frequently quite affordable. There's no shame in silver rather than gold. Don't rule out upper-end costume jewelry either, a whimsical cloisonné pin, or a few bangles for her wrist. Earrings offer limitless choices, from tiny porcelain elephants to huge colored hoops. *Caveat:* You might want to give jewelry sparingly, on special occasions only, lest you start feeling pressured to up the ante; after months of no-occasion gold, a birthday calls for rubies. Of course, if you're wealthy and can afford it …

5. *Do a Strip Tease For Her.* Women are always stripping for men, in public or private – and guess what? Stripping gets women hot too! Put on some slow saxophone jazz. Take your time. Touch yourself in key locations. Tease her mercilessly. Use your imagination. If you need help, classes on stripping for both genders are available in some big cities.

6. *Mid-Week Getaway.* Without telling her, reserve the swankiest suite at the swankiest hotel that's reasonably convenient for an overnight stay. Stock the room with champagne and strawberries, little treats to eat, flowers. Be sure she's free on the day you've chosen to do this; perhaps make plans with her beforehand. Then call her during the day and tell her to meet you in the hotel bar for a drink. At some point during drinks, simply place the key to the suite in front of her.

7. *Hunt Her Down.* Tell her not to wear underwear beneath her skirt while she goes out shopping, either in and out of street stores or to a mall. Let her know that while she walks around, you'll be following, and you want her to subtly tease you – throw back her hair, hike up her skirt, cast meaningful looks over her shoulder. *Caveat*: Only try this if you know it's something she'll enjoy – remember, this is *her* surprise, not yours!

8. *Give Her a Bonus.* Assuming Sugar Baby gets a regular allowance, once in awhile tack some extra cash onto it; the amount depends on your budget. Or leave a check somewhere in her house – on her pillow, or in her (empty) coffee pot. Random bonuses are a welcome surprise, and a holiday bonus is plain good sense – after all, when everyone else is getting big Christmas bonuses, you don't want Baby to be left out or feel deprived!

9. *Give Her a Raise.* Even the Feds raised the minimum wage last year, after a decade of stagnation. Sugar Baby shouldn't have to wait that long; in fact, after your first six months together it's a good idea to raise her allowance. Don't make a big deal of it: don't ask for new perks in

exchange, or talk about it beforehand. Just give it to her with a note explaining it's permanent, and tell her why (an opportunity to give her verbal kudos).

10. *Give Her A Credit Card.* If you haven't done so already, give Sugar Baby her own credit card. A cap on the line of credit is perfectly okay; just don't make it pitifully low (under $3000 would be low). If she already has a credit card...give her another one! Or, instead of a major card, give her one from a specialty shop or boutique she particularly likes.

What If You O.D.?

Sugar is a potent substance. It can carry you off to Elysian Fields, then toss you right back into stark reality. It's easily abused, insinuating itself into every part of your life, body and soul, so that you crave sweetness even to the exclusion of balance and good health. Some people run after the Sugar rush like junkies chasing the dragon. They can't give it up if they try.

Then again, why give up a good thing?

Sometimes Sugar arrangements turn out so well they evolve into more than part-time fun and games. When both partners in a Sugar relationship find themselves falling in love, they've overdosed. Unlike real sugar or drug overdose, however, this addiction is not only manageable, but can turn out to be wonderful.

> I first met Adam when I was 28. He was my Sugar Daddy for two years, and the relationship just kept getting better and better. We moved in together; then he proposed. Twelve years later here we are. I never would have predicted this, but one thing's for sure, we couldn't be happier. And I probably never would have met him outside of the Sugar Daddy thing, you know? Life is so weird.

This story is less uncommon than you might think. It makes perfect sense, though: in a long-term Sugar relationship two people spend a great deal of time together, get to know each other well, and make love on a regular, increasingly satisfying, basis. Add to this the Sugar principles that guarantee the giving and receiving of pleasure, and love cannot be too far off.

Of course, not every Sugar arrangement has this potential. Some people are more disciplined than others. They're careful to keep a lid on their emotions, setting limits such as seeing each other less frequently and for shorter periods of time, so they never get close enough to fall in love. Some are so determined to keep the NSA going they simply don't let themselves go anywhere near love's complications.

For those who do allow the sweetness to get even sweeter, the possibilities are vast. How convenient, to already know someone intimately for two years, like the woman in the above post, before jumping into a committed relationship. Actually it's less like jumping and more about going forward. This is no love at first sight! The romantic myths that so often damage relationships haven't gotten a foothold in this one. In that sense, a Sugar relationship may have an even better chance at success than one that starts off conventionally.

Should you and your Sugar OD, and you're comfortable following your bliss, *mazel tov!* The only real problem is: What will you tell your grandkids when they ask you how you met?

On the other hand, if you and your Sugar OD and you're a hundred percent certain you positively honestly for sure don't want it to continue, you'll probably have to give up Sugar – or at least *this* Sugar – completely. It's difficult, if not impossible, to go backwards once you've crossed this particular border. The comfortable rhythms and easy flow you two shared prior to this development can be ruined by it. Yes, it's a sad thing to face – but it's not the end of the world.

In the next chapter we'll address the ways a Sugar relationship can go sour, and what to do about it.

"We can go into any store
you want...except this one!"

CHAPTER TWELVE:

WHEN THE SUGAR SOURS

All good things come to an end, and Sugar relationships are no exception. We've heard of some that last a good long time – ten or twelve years – while others fizzle out in a few months. The ending of a relationship is as much a part of it as the beginning and middle; considering that it's the intention of Sugar relationships to do things differently from the conventional, then attention must be paid to the way they end. It is not inevitable that break-ups be violent, nasty, or devastating. If we can imagine them differently, perhaps we can make them so.

There's probably no way out of the natural sadness that comes with any loss except by going through it, but piling on more misery is unnecessary. If a couple can manage, during the difficult break-up phase, not to destroy all the good feelings they've had for each other, they might even be able to remain friends – though it's best not to have that expectation. Friendship between ex-lovers is, most of the time, extraordinarily difficult, and forcing it will only increase the pressure on everyone. The focus and goal of the break-up phase should be to *minimize negative feelings* in order to salvage, if not a friendship, at least one's positive memories, undistorted by a toxic and/or violent end. (Those further evolved might also use this time for self-examination and knowledge, but for most people, a graceful exit is enough to strive for.)

Some Sugar Babies and Daddies feel more comfortable setting up the ending right at the beginning of the relationship. One Sugar Daddy had such a hard time with the break-up of his first Sugar Baby relationship that on his next go-round he decided to address the end at the outset.

> I set up a little six–month trust that would kick in the minute I ended my second relationship, and I told my second Baby about it going in. It's worked beautifully. Now we can be friends. I highly recommend it.

Opinion in the Sugar community varies widely on this subject. Some people don't like the idea of pre-determining an ending, and think it should be allowed to evolve organically. Those who do like the idea, though, say that, theoretically, if a time frame for the relationship has already been negotiated, it will be a kinder, gentler process rather than a sudden, traumatic split. Theoretically.

For instance, say Sugar Baby is a student who wants Daddy to cover her tuition for six months: they might decide to designate that as the time period of their arrangement. If this seems too short a time, they can leave themselves a loophole by agreeing simply to re-visit negotiations after six months, then decide if they want to continue or not. The ability to negotiate honest, clear–cut agreements is key to creating and maintaining the ultimate Sugar arrangement; if Sugar Daddies and Babies master these skills, they can be applied to any issue, even the break-up. It's true, as the naysayers point out, that planning for a breakup is more practical than romantic – but we warned you going in: This is not about romance. Would you prefer *"the conversation with the flying plates"*[2*] as a break-up strategy?

To some extent *how* a couple breaks up depends on *why*: some whys are more tolerable than others. For instance, if Sugar Daddy must relocate for business, Baby probably won't be as hurt or angry as if he falls in love with someone else. The reasons for endings to Sugar arrangements are as varied as the people in them, and include the same ones as all relationships do, plus a few that are unique to the Sugar lifestyle.

Conventional reasons include: one person meets and prefers someone new; someone's moving out of Dodge; boredom; craving the adventure only a new lover can bring; a betrayal of trust or an unforgivable act (unforgivable by *the other person*, that is; nothing is inherently unforgivable); a pile-up of little and big irritations; failure to communicate or miscommunication; a problem that's lain

---

2 * from *I Wish I Were In Love Again*, Richard Rodgers composer

dormant all along comes to the surface; some quality or behavior by one person that the other one never liked worsens over time, until tolerance for it snaps like a worn-out rubber band.

Breakup Reasons Unique to Sugar Relationships

- The wife finds out.

- Sugar Daddy demands that Baby be monogamous, even if he isn't and it wasn't in their agreement, and she refuses.

  > Sugar Daddies always want to be The Only One, so I let them believe they are. I feel kind of bad for lying, but when I met two SDs I liked, I figured, why not? And I'm becoming close friends with both of them. I guess I understand, but if I wanted monogamy, possessiveness, and jealousy, I'd be in a traditional relationship.

- Sugar Baby gets involved in a conventional relationship.

  > I decided to end an arrangement because of jealousy. Just because I had a Sugar Daddy didn't mean I was putting my love life on hold. I'm very marriage-minded, and I was looking for someone all the time I was in a Sugar relationship. When I started dating my boyfriend things got odd between me and my SD - he was too jealous, and I couldn't deal with it. After all, I wasn't jealous of his wife.

- Sugar Daddy feels neglected for other reasons.

  > I'm thinking of breaking things off with my Sugar Baby. She's unreliable and her schedule never works out with mine. She never sees me on the weekend because she'd rather go out and party with her friends. She never has dinner or spends more than two hours with me. I know I don't own her, and she deserves to have a life of her own, but SB's need to prioritize. We SD's pay their rent, their credit card bills, car payments, and in some cases tuition. We do not belong on the bottom of the list.

- Sugar Baby wants more money, or feels she's not getting enough "mutual benefits."

> My SD relationship ended when I felt I wasn't getting any benefits. Instead of complicating things by talking to my Sugar Daddy about why he kept forgetting my allowance, and other issues, I just ended it.

- Negotiations were never completely satisfying to one or both people, and long-buried resentment comes to the surface.

Then there are some truly heinous situations endemic to the nature of the Sugar arrangement.

- One person threatens the other. Says the SeekingArrangement Blogmaster:

> When a Sugar Daddy told his Sugar Baby of a few weeks that he'd decided to end their relationship, the vengeful girl told him to reconsider or risk having their intimate conversations sent to every fax machine in the company where he was a CEO. Similarly, we have heard of numerous tales from Sugar Babies who can't get a stalking suitor off their backs.

- Without warning, Baby blackmails Sugar Daddy: if he doesn't give her X, Y or Z, she says, she'll rat him out to family or work.

Why would a Sugar Baby do something like this? Maybe she was dissatisfied with the amount of money she agreed to, or maybe during the course of the relationship she decides she's worth more; either way, Daddy turns down her request for a raise and she wants revenge. Or maybe she's a con artist who's been planning to blackmail him all along – a scam Daddy never saw coming. Then again, she might just be bitchy, quirky, off her meds or off her rocker.

- Sugar Daddy turns into a stalker.

When this happens it's usually after a breakup, or when Baby refuses to give Sugar Daddy something he requests. Or maybe he was never that happy with the terms of their agreement. Or, again, maybe he planned it all along and/or he's your garden variety psycho. Whatever the reason, he begins to follow her around, spying on her, trying to catch her cheating, bothering her everywhere she goes. He calls her at all hours of the day or night, even at work, and grills her like it's the Spanish Inquisition. He shows up unannounced, even drunk, enraged if she doesn't drop everything for him. He becomes violent.

• Sugar Baby becomes the stalker.

Instead of hounding Sugar Daddy, though, she targets his wife. She might call the woman, send her letters, visit the house pretending to be someone else, or direct all kinds of irrational acts towards his family. Bunny homicide is sometimes involved.

Certainly these terrible behaviors can and have occurred in all sorts of relationship configurations – but Sugar arrangements, because they aren't long-term commitments, they involve money, and they sometimes require secrecy, are more susceptible than most.

Finally, alternative lifestyles seem to attract a high proportion of people who are emotionally unstable. Remember, however, that there are laws against crimes like blackmail, violence, and stalking. Should you become a victim of these or any other crimes, you should report them to law enforcement authorities.

Ending on a Sweet Note: Fifty Ways to Leave

If gay men are the pros of Daddy fantasy, gay women have the breakup market cornered. Lesbians have refined the breakup process to a high art, with long periods of time devoted to processing emotions. There are a lot of reasons for this: to state the obvious, lesbians are women, and women generally place a high value on emotions. Women also tend to be intense about friendship: there's a do-or-die quality to girlhood friendships that can sometimes border on obsession. Because it's so important to them, many lesbians try to remain friends with their ex-lovers.

Lesbian Nation has grown over the past few decades, with lovers turning into friends and vice versa. Overlapping chains of friends, lovers, ex-lovers, and wanna-be lovers often form close-knit circles of social and emotional support. With all their experience, lesbians have a thing or two to teach us about breaking up. How do they do it? And just how successful are they?

The first thing required to achieve a good ending is to simply be present: if this matters, then attention must be paid. That means talking and listening to what the other person has to say, and hearing the pain, anger, and disappointment that things didn't work out as hoped. This is not easy: with each person experiencing some or all of these feelings, they can easily be overwhelmed. Upon learning of resentments we didn't know about, we tend to feel guilty and get defensive. It sounds crazy, or at the very least like a bad joke, but a lot of lesbians enter therapy solely to deal with the breakup. And if you do choose to remain friends, the story doesn't end – it goes right on generating more emotions! Now you know why lesbians are always tired.

I'm not recommending that every couple see a therapist to handle a breakup, especially not of a relationship that was supposed to be NSA. I'm just pointing out the effort is sometimes required for a positive ending.

The Ultimate Horrible Break-Up

Everything horrible that can possibly happen during a breakup happens in *The Breakup*, with Vince Vaughn and Jennifer Aniston. They remain living under the same roof for months, torturing one another in ways large and small. He invites the guys over for loud beer-soaked poker parties. She parades her dates around the condo. Most of the time they don't communicate, at least not directly or positively, except to fight. They say cruel, hurtful things to one another. They distort and destroy every shred of good they had and any love they shared before things changed. A year later, when they meet by chance on the street, the regret and pain they feel towards one another is palpable. It's clear these people are going to live with that regret for the rest of their lives.

This is not a breakup anyone in their right mind would want – and yet it's what happens, more or less, to many, if not most, couples. Avoiding the patterns played out in *The Breakup* takes self-discipline and impulse control.

Things to Avoid During a Breakup

During the ending phase of a relationship, certain behavior should be avoided like the plague. Both people should agree not to engage in the following behaviors:

- Character Assassination
- The Blame Game
- Ignoring each other
- Pretending not to care
- Confessing past secrets and sins
- Flaunting new lovers, new friends or a new lifestyle

- Drinking or doing drugs around each other
- Dragging other people into the breakup, asking them to take sides
- Trashing each other's possessions
- Violence, cops, murder and mayhem

Now that you know what not to do, here are some ideas to put into practice that will, hopefully, make for a sweeter – even if it's a bittersweet – ending.

- Schedule time to talk things over during long walks or meals. Tell each other whatever needs telling: your reasons for ending, feelings that may have been kept under wraps, what if any kind of connection you want to maintain.
- Don't rush it. Allow as much time as it takes for the process to complete itself. Plan specific dates and times to talk. Some lesbian couples take weeks or even months to go through the process.
- If the process deteriorates, don't force it. If talking reverts to accusations, yelling, tears, etc., take a break. Don't see each other for a few weeks. Letting go of a relationship happens in stages, and the old saying *Time Heals* is accurate: the natural passage of time helps to move things along; intensity gets dialed back a little bit more each time you talk.
- Move On. Other events and activities will eventually supplant a preoccupation with the relationship. Both people will hopefully move on with their lives, until one day they'll realize there's nothing left to talk about. Break out the champagne!

Relationships for the 21st Century

Now that you've managed a sweet ending complete with champagne, it's time to get back on the horse – you know, when you fall off a horse you're supposed to get right back on, broken bones and all. Likewise, after you've tasted Sugar gone sour, the thing to do is sit down at your desk, fire up the computer, and click your way over to SeekingArrangement.com.

Common wisdom has it that people need time off between love affairs to regroup and recharge. Generally that's good advice – but since it usually takes time, even as much as a year, to find the right Sugar Baby or Daddy, it makes sense to begin the hunt right away. By the time something materializes you'll be more than ready for it. Besides, one goal of Sugar arrangements is to minimize emotional wounds so that licking them doesn't become a full-time avocation.

It'll be easier to find and choose a Sugar sweetheart the second or third or fourth time around – by now you're a pro. Even if your experience was for some reason limited – the relationship was brief, you spent very little time together, intimacy never went that deep – by reading this book you've learned more about Sugar dating. At least I hope you did. I hope this has been helpful as a guide, and that it's shown how to make Sugar arrangements as, or more, satisfying as conventional ones. I hope this book encourages more people to take a dip in the Sugar bowl.

Why? Because Sugar arrangements may prove to be the ultimate relationship configuration for the 21st century.

At the time of this writing, we are less than a decade into a new millennium. The world is entirely different here in the

21st century than at any other time in history. While that is true of every era, it's more extreme in ours, due to rapid-fire technological development along with ever increasing scientific discoveries about the human brain, genetics, and behavior. We are standing on the cusp of something new, something that might be extraordinary or devastating, depending on how we deal with the experience. For all we know, alternative kinds of relationships will ultimately lead to new conventions: today's alternatives are tomorrow's norms.

Back in the first chapter I talked about old-fashioned arranged marriages.

These were, and continue to be seen by some cultures, as the natural order of the universe (the same way that Western society sees monogamous marriage). The purpose of arranged marriage was and is to strengthen a family's holdings, whether they are farms, lands, corporations or bloodlines. Negotiations are not just for the benefit of the individuals, but for the families involved.

Today's emphasis on the individual, so pronounced in Western culture, is gaining global legitimacy at a time when new possibilities, thanks to technology and the Internet, are expanding. Sugar websites and the Sugar community make it possible for people to manage their own arrangements without the assistance and control of family members, fostering greater self-sufficiency – not the self-sufficiency of isolation and hyper individualism, but the kind that occurs in social networks like Facebook and My Space, and on interactive blogs and bulletin boards. In these online communities, individuals successfully accomplish their own goals, whether it's making friends or finding a job – but always within the context of, and an acknowledged need for, a connection to the group.

Sugar arrangements are the ideal model for this milieu, rewarding the people involved and extending their individual reach or "holdings," whatever these might be. In this environment of open experimentation, Sugar arrangements, or some variation thereof, may turn out to be the standard for the 21st century.

WHAT TO SPEND YOUR EXTRA CASH ON...

CHAPTER THIRTEEN:

IS A SUGAR ARRANGEMENT RIGHT FOR YOU?

Now that you know your way around the Sugar Bowl, and you're armed with more information than you're likely to need, you should be able to make a well-informed decision: *Is this kind of arrangement right for you?* In this last chapter we'll help you answer that question from the standpoint of four considerations: emotional, social, moral, and, last but certainly not least, financial. Your part is to conduct a self-inventory, as you read, of each of these categories as they relate to you. By the time you're through, you should be fairly certain whether the Sugar lifestyle suits you – or not.

Emotional Snafus

From an emotional standpoint, certain personality types adapt better to the Sugar lifestyle than others. For instance, if you tend to get very attached to someone, to the point where you're clingy and demanding, a Sugar arrangement probably won't work for you. On the other hand, if you're emotionally independent – you like (sometimes even prefer) spending time alone, you don't obsess about where your lover is or with whom, and you don't need to be with a lover in order to feel complete – then this kind of relationship is perfect for you. Between these two poles lie a range of characteristics and behaviors that indicate whether you're capable of separating emotions from intimacy. At first glance that might strike some people, particularly women, as an oxymoron, impossible to achieve and perhaps even undesirable. But let's look at the components of the phrase, *separate emotions from intimacy,* more carefully.

Emotions are feelings that come and go in time: one minute we might feel joyful; a few minutes later something happens to plunge us into depression. One aspect of maturity is the ability to experience a wide range of emotions without allowing them to rule our behavior. When we allow our emotions to define us this way, we're apt to run into trouble. Feelings are transitory and, as such, are not a solid foundation on which to base major life decisions – or even small ones.

I know a woman who puts her beloved house on the market every time the basement floods; but as soon as the problem's resolved, she changes her mind – once she was even sued by someone who'd put down a deposit in between my friend's shifting moods. When she learned to base her decisions on logical thought instead of on momentary emotional distress, she recognized that she didn't want to sell her house, and resolved the basement problem once and for all. The moral of this story: we cannot base decisions on feelings because they could change at any moment. A mature person knows we don't have to act on every emotion that passes through us.

People often confuse *intimacy* with emotion. Actually, intimacy is a quality, or an atmosphere, of closeness between two people, generated by mutual experiences, or by spending long periods of time together; deep conversation can create intimacy, as can a brief but intense occurrence like a plane crash: we're liable to feel extremely close to a stranger who pulls us out of the wreckage of a plane.

The most common path to intimacy is sex. We frequently find genuine intimacy with sex partners and mistake it for something permanent – but as Susie *Sexpert* Bright points out, we can have rip-roarin', satisfying, and intimate sex with someone without wanting to share so much as an ice cream cone afterwards, much less get married and raise a family. Again, major life decisions based on fleeting emotions can equal major life mistakes.

When we learn to distinguish between intimacy and emotional response, we've gone a long way toward making our relationships calmer and more manageable: we reap the benefits of intimacy without the storms and craziness that often accompany intense emotions.

If you can separate emotions from intimacy, then you've passed an important benchmark in this process. Still, there are yet more potential snafus on the road to a successful Sugar arrangement.

If you're a woman who's considering becoming a Sugar Baby, and you've had negative experiences with men in the past, an arrangement free of the demands of commitment can be extremely liberating. On the other hand, the Sugar lifestyle might be disturbing for you. You could find yourself comparing every potential Sugar Daddy to a partner who cheated on you. You might feel contempt, consciously or not, for a married Sugar Daddy. If you haven't yet forgiven – or forgotten – the pain of a lover's infidelity, you could end up reliving it over and over again with a Sugar Daddy. If this is the case, then a Sugar arrangement may not be the best dating choice for you.

(*Caveat*: ANY woman who has strong negative feelings towards adulterous married men, whether from personal experience or not, should not choose a Sugar Daddy from the married column. Most of the marrieds do tell the truth about their status in their profiles – and besides, more single than married men are registered on SeekingArrangment.com.)

If you're a man who's thinking of becoming a Sugar Daddy, and your past is littered with broken-hearted or angry women you've mistreated, be forewarned: the Sugar lifestyle is *not* about taking advantage of women, despite the female-as-victim stereotype. *Au contraire*: the ideal Sugar Daddy treats his Sugar Baby like a queen. He genuinely *wants* to help and care for her, and he doesn't hold a death grip on the purse strings. If, however, he squeezes those dollar Joes "until that eagle grins," and frets like a thrifty pioneer housewife about *wasting money*, he's not the kind of guy likely to have a good experience on

SeekingArrangement.com – nor are potential Sugar Babies apt to respond positively to him.

In the long view, this kind of guy is in danger of becoming a bitter old man, if he isn't already; a classic Ebenezer Scrooge. By limiting his spending rather than freely enjoying his wealth, he's doing the exact opposite of what he set out to do as a young man, i.e., make pots of money with which to enjoy life to the max. The Sugar Daddy lifestyle is an opportunity for men to do the things they worked hard all their lives to deserve and afford. If they can't enjoy it, they're bound to feel like their life's work was a waste of time, and rightly so.

Unless a man comes into this lifestyle with a generous heart and the expectation of good times with women *as equal companions*, then this lifestyle won't work. If, on the other hand, you're able to spend money without bitterness or resentment, recognizing that nobody's trying to take advantage of you here, then SeekingArrangement. com is a big, fabulous playground.

Social Ramifications

Early in this book we talked about mainstream attitudes towards Sugar Arrangements, the stigma and uninformed judgments conventional people hold for those who dare to live an alternative lifestyle. If you've spent most of your life among the conventional, it may be difficult for you to stand up to the judgments of friends and family, or even strangers. Though stereotypes about Sugar Daddies and Sugar Babies are slowly changing, most people still think this is just another way for men to exploit women, who they see as perilously young victims and/or empty-headed bimbos. If you're easily influenced by other people's opinions, or if it bothers you to be thought of in such a negative way, social attitudes can be another obstacle.

If, on the other hand, you've lived a somewhat less conventional life, or you've done a bit of relationship experimentation, and/or you don't pay much attention to what other people think, then what other people say shouldn't stop you from having fun in the Sugar Bowl.

There is a third option: you might be living a conventional life, you might suffer over people's opinions of you – and you just might make a conscious decision to break through these barriers. Some people make the choice to change their attitudes and behavior, to live the way they want to live without caring what their mother, cousin or best friend thinks of it. When you free yourself in this way, it doesn't mean you don't care about the people close to you – it just means you care about yourself more.

Not everyone, however, can rebel successfully. Some people who choose this path never entirely get past their sadness for the people they've lost along the way – but that doesn't necessarily mean they regret the choice. Social rebellion is not an easy path, and it's not for everyone. It's up to you to figure out if this is the path you want to follow. As Robert Frost said, with much sadness but little regret, *I took the road less traveled by / and that has made all the difference.*

Moral Dilemmas

Whether based on religion, sociology, or philosophy, your ideas about morality can make or break your ability to enjoy a Sugar arrangement. Whether this lifestyle causes you moral discomfort also depends somewhat on your current lifestyle, specifically, your marital status – or the status of your partner-in-sugar-crime. For most people, adultery is the big moral consideration in Sugar arrangements – but there may be others.

At SeekingArrangement.com we take no formal position on moral issues, including adultery. We do understand, however, that moral concerns are not to be scoffed at or lightly dismissed.

In Eastern philosophy the concept of *karma* applies primarily to reincarnation – but *karma* can also operate within one lifetime, as in the biblical, *as ye sow so shall ye reap.* Some who live by this credo don't engage in activities they deem immoral, even when tempted. Others go against their beliefs and act on their desires, shouldering a heavy guilt burden; sometimes they regret their behavior, and suffer so much inner turmoil they "confess" as a way to relieve their conscience. This only compounds the original mistake, in that they hurt someone else.

If you strongly believe in *karma*, or in a Christian heaven and hell, or in any code of morality that sheds judgment on Sugar relationships (married or not), then this lifestyle may not be right for you. Again, this is something only you yourself can know, and if you're not sure, you'll need to look inside yourself. It may even be that you *think* you don't have moral issues, but once you embark on a Sugar relationship you discover you really do, and, further, that they're genuinely *yours,* not just something imposed from the outside. On the other hand, you could discover the reverse, and that you don't really believe in what you thought you did. Whatever your decision, it should be respected, most of all by you. It would be a mistake to force yourself to do something that makes you feel immoral, sinful, or at risk of putting your soul in jeopardy. It's not the end of the world if you can't live a Sugar lifestyle – after all, there's always fantasy. As Sly and the Family Stone put it, *Don't you know you are free? Well at least in your mind if you want to be.*

Respecting a person's moral code doesn't mean we agree with it. Everyone lives by their own morality. Some conscious and caring people take the Golden Rule as their only moral code – *Do unto others as you would have others do unto you* – and that's *it*. Except for hurting others, anything goes – particularly with regard to their personal sex lives. For those people, a Sugar arrangement between consenting adults presents no moral conflict. We respect everyone's right to live by his or her own belief system.

What we do not respect, or more accurately don't *endorse*, is living in a way (unless circumstances make it unavoidable) that maximizes conflict and turmoil, whether manifested in outer chaos or internal suffering. Life is too short to make oneself or others unnecessarily miserable. This is why, when deciding about a sugar arrangement, you need to take your own moral standards into consideration.

Financial Considerations

Can you afford to be a Sugar Daddy…or a Sugar Mommy?

Success in the Sugar Bowl – i.e., finding a great Sugar Baby, spending time with her, having fun, doing things (all kinds of things) together – can only occur if Sugar Daddy or Mommy (a) has enough money to spend without neglecting other responsibilities; and (b) has fun/enjoys/derives pleasure from spending it on a Sugar Baby, and does so without any qualms or resentment.

Case Study # 1 Joe the truck driver:

Remember the truck driver who called when I was a guest on the Playboy Radio Channel? Let's call him Joe, Case Study #1 in our financial inventory. When Joe called in and asked if it was realistic for someone like him, a regular working man who drives a truck, to have a Sugar Baby, I asked him a few questions before answering.

Brandon Wade (BW): What do you want to get out of Sugar Daddy dating? An occasional but reliable fling? Or a live-in Sugar Baby to be available, more or less, whenever you need her?

Joe: Something in-between. Since I'm on the road all week, I can only spend weekends with her – but with everything else I do too, it wouldn't be the whole weekend. Maybe just Friday and Saturday nights, going out to dinner and dancing, or to see a movie. I don't like casual sex, it would have to be real, intimate. If I could find a woman who's open to a real relationship, but with certain limits and no strings...

BW: That's certainly do-able. Besides paying for dates and giving her a regular allowance, would you also give her surprise gifts once in awhile, or an occasional splurge at the mall? Would you pay a bill now and then if she wanted you to?

Joe: I don't know if I can afford all that!

BW: Don't worry, you don't have to do all of it – but just so you know, most Sugar Babies like to be pampered, at least a little, with an occasional present or a cash bonus surprise – if you can only do an allowance-based arrangement, your pool of Sugar Baby matches will be somewhat limited. Before we jump to any conclusions, though, let's see exactly what you can afford. What's your annual income?

Joe: I make $ 75,000 a year.

BW: What's that a month, after taxes? Around $4,200, right?

Joe: Just about.

BW: And what are your monthly expenses?

Joe: Give me a minute here. (Joe figures out his budget.) My mortgage is $1,000.00, other monthly fixed expenses come to around $1,000. I put $400 a month into my retirement plan. The remaining is my disposable income.

BW: It looks to me like you have around $1,700 left over every month. If she agrees to a $1,000 monthly allowance, you could use the other $700 for pampering expenses – paying some of her bills, spontaneous gifts, a trip to the mall. So, Joe, I'd say you're in good shape to be a Sugar Daddy. Go get your Sugar Baby!

Most men, I realize, know how to calculate a budget, and can figure things out without this example, but in case you're uncertain, the above is a suggested formula. Don't jump into the Sugar Bowl without knowing for certain you can afford it – going broke here could be a disaster.

Bill the CEO: Case Study # 2

Our second Case Study is Bill, the CEO of a Fortune 500 company. Bill is on a whole different level from Joe – but although he earns a lot more money, he has major responsibilities, including a wife and three pre-college kids. He didn't want to take on Sugar Daddy expenses without being certain he could manage it without short-changing his family.

Bill makes $600,000 per year, or about $30,000 per month after taxes. Mortgage and taxes for his $2.5 million dollar home are about $12,000 a month. His fixed expenses, which include payments and insurance for three high end cars and a Harley Davidson, allowance for his stay at home wife, private school tuition and college savings accounts for all three kids, total another $15,000 per month. In addition to his regular monthly expenses, he has to budget $2,500 for unexpected events, such as a spontaneous weekend at his lake house, veterinary bills, or entertaining friends and colleagues. After totaling these up, he has $500 left over – barely enough to cover an allowance, much less any frills for a Sugar Baby. I told Bill that unless he gives up his third car or his motorcycle, he should steer clear of a sugar arrangement.

In Conclusion

If, after reading this chapter, you still have qualms or questions, you should delay your first visit to SeekingArrangement.com, if not cancel the idea altogether. But if you've come to the conclusion that a Sugar arrangement would suit you just fine – then welcome to SeekingArrangement.com, and congratulations on having chosen to take this exciting new journey.

We only live once, and that one life is short to boot. With so many places to go, people to meet, and experiences to be had, we all want to maximize the quality of our time on earth, to live life to the fullest. That's what this book, and the Sugar lifestyle, is all about: helping people live life to the max, making wonderful human connections, and taking a chance on alternatives. While this may not be for everyone, if it is for you, then use this book as a guide, and come experience this lifestyle for yourself. I am offering readers an exclusive free trial membership on SeekingArrangement.com. To redeem this offer, please visit the following website and follow the registration instructions: http://www.seekingarrangement.com/book/offer.php.

Welcome to the Sugar Bowl, and good luck! May all your relationships be sweet.

GLOSSARY

Arm Candy: A gorgeous (and delicious) young female (or male) whose purpose is primarily ornamental.

Beard: A female (or male) escort for the opposite sex obscuring the fact that the person they are escorting is gay or lesbian.

Bobcat: Refers to a woman in her 30's who sexually pursues younger men.

Boy Toy: Refers to a young boy or man in a relationship with an older woman or man. Use of this terminology is considered by some to be impolite.

Candy-Leg: Synonym for Sugar Daddy. Refers to a wealthy, older man who supports or contributes to the support of a young woman.

Cougar: Refers to an older woman, usually in her 40's or well kept 50's, who sexually pursues younger men, or, in the case of a Lesbian Cougar, younger women.

Doughed-Up Darling: Dated synonym for Sugar Daddy from the early 1900s. Refers to a young woman who accepts money and gifts from older men in return for companionship or sex.

Geisha: Traditional, female Japanese entertainers, whose skills include performing various Japanese arts, such as classical music and dance. Contrary to popular western belief, geisha are not prostitutes.

Gigolo: A man supported by a woman, usually in return for his attentions; a professional male escort or companion to women.

Gold Digger: Refers to a relationship in which a young person pursues an older person solely for monetary gain.

Hetaera: A companion to men in ancient Greece, one of a class of very highly cultivated courtesans prized for her intellect.

Internet Dating Terms:

WF: White Female.

MWF: Married White Female.

BM: Black Male.

MWM: Married White Male.

WM: White Male.

Jailbait: Refers to a particularly sexually attractive person, female or male, below the legal age of consent. This designation connotes enticement to endanger oneself by being prosecuted for statutory rape.

Kept Woman: A female lover who is financially "kept," whose living expenses are paid for by a man (or woman in the case of lesbians).

Lolita: Refers to a sexually precocious young girl who is the object of desire of a significantly older man. The term derives from the title character of Vladimir Nabokov's novel *Lolita*, referred to by the narrator as a nymphet. While "nymphet" is still used to refer to children, "Lolita" has come to be applied to older adolescents and young women in the context of pornography. In South America, "Lolita" is slang for a prostitute, a usage unrelated to Nabokov's novel.

May-December Romance: Refers to a general and non-prejudicial expression for an age-disparate relationship. The expression draws an implicit analogy between one's lifetime and the time of year. Thus "May" refers to the younger partner, who is in the spring of his or her life. "December" is the elder partner, in the winter of his or her life.

MILF: (*Mom I'd Like to Fuck*): Refers to mothers who attract the sexual attention of high-school boys. This acronym was popularized by the movie *American Pie*. The term may also stand for *Mama Is Looking Fine*.

Mistress: The "other" woman in a love triangle, usually the illicit lover of a married man.

Mrs. Robinson: Derives from the movie *The Graduate*; Refers to an older woman romantically involved with a younger man.

NSA: No-strings Attached. Refers to a relationship where there is no emotional commitment. You are free to date or see other people.

Robbing the Cradle (also known as Cradle Snatching): Refers to a situation in which an older individual seduces a much younger one; the term stigmatizes the act through its use of the word "robbing." The tone of this phrase is highly situational—in some cases, where the consensual nature of the relationship is clear, it is often used in a jesting manner, but where the consensual nature may not be evident, it can be intended in a pejorative sense. People who "rob the cradle" are commonly called "cradle snatchers" or "cradle robbers."

Robbing the Grave: May refer to the opposite of "Robbing the Cradle." Here the object of affection is an older person.

Samurai Women: Maintaining the household was the main duty of samurai women. This was especially crucial during early feudal Japan, when warrior husbands were often traveling abroad or engaged in clan battles.

Sugar Daddy: A man who provides financial, professional, or other forms of support to an individual in exchange for personal benefit (e.g., intimacy, companionship, etc.).

Sugar Baby: An individual who provides intimacy, companionship, or other forms of attention to a Sugar Daddy or Sugar Mama in exchange for personal benefit (e.g., financial support, professional advancement, etc).

Sugar Mama (or Mommy): Refers to a wealthy, usually older woman, who offers money or gifts to a less wealthy, usually younger, person in return for companionship or sexual favors.

Sugartit: An old fashioned cloth and sugar water pacifier for an infant; for an adult, support they have grown accustomed to from a Sugar Daddy or Sugar Mama.

Walker: An attractive younger male companion (usually gay) who escorts an older woman to a high profile event.

Diary of a Sugar Baby
by American Geisha

<u>Day One</u>

After eight years of post-divorce dating trauma, I'd had enough, and decided to search for a Sugar Daddy on SeekingArrangement. com. It's the perfect situation for me - I like having a man to give affection to, get financial assistance from, enjoy and explore my sexuality with, and expect nothing else beyond a mutual enjoyment of each other. I don't have to worry if he has poor personal hygiene, or leaves things on the bathroom counter, or if we have different tastes in home decorating – he always leaves. He won't get frustrated if I don't make the bed or do the dishes or have dinner ready when he wants it. And I've come to appreciate the luxury of sleeping diagonally across the bed.

But how do I tell these potential Sugar Daddies that I'm interesting, intelligent, fun and attractive? Most importantly, how do I do it differently than all the other beautiful women on the site? I pore over picture after picture taken by family, friends and ex-boyfriend, but none of them show me the way I look now. I pull out the digital camera, put on a provocative little white dress and turn my backside to the camera. This *is* a Sugar Daddy search, after all. Pleasures of the body are involved – but I want to come across as intriguing and classy, not blatant. The profile should be short, tell just enough to encourage a curiosity to know more.

What I seek…let's see…intelligence, humor, sexual fun and a strong, successful man. The picture and profile are up and I'm in the pool. Let's see who swims by.

Day Two

My world has just expanded from a small town to the entire United States: on the first day 30 men have looked at my profile. I had no idea. And so many of them seem interesting, and match what I'm looking for. This is going to be fun.

Day Three

I've started email conversations with several potential Sugar Daddies. Although most don't have a photo, I like getting to know their personality first.

One gentleman assures me he has all his teeth and doesn't live with Mom. Good start! Still, he brings a smile to my face by saying he's sincere and romantic. Hmmmm...email sent.

Then there's the sweet young man who has one home in the Midwest and another on the coast, very close to me. Tempting - but his picture shows a rivulet of wine running down his bare chest as he pours it from a shoe. I prefer my wine in a glass, thank you very much. Besides, good wine should *never* be wasted by pouring it over a body, no matter how attractive it is.

Then there's the extremely successful businessman who wants a dominant woman so he can lick her toes and wear certain undergarments in places they don't belong. Sorry, that would probably provoke a severe fit of the giggles from me where *they* don't belong – in the bedroom.

A very tempting offer from a man who wants me to meet him at a local restaurant and pretend I'm there for a job interview. He tells me what to wear and how to present myself. Hmm…could be fun; but when I ask about the arrangement, he tells me to send pictures showing more skin before we discuss it. Sorry, but I need to know you're serious about something other than looking at my pictures.

Day Four

Several email conversations progress to phone calls. The conversations flow easily, and chemistry develops with a couple of the men. We set up times to get together.

My first meeting is with a Sugar Daddy who claims to be a rogue. He is almost certainly that. An international businessman, he has homes in Europe and California, with ladies in many countries; he's seeking two or three to take care of and spend time with. Now, *this* sounds interesting! He's even attractive. I'm already picking out the date ensemble. He volunteers to charter a plane to meet me in my home town, but since I'm going to be in his neighborhood anyway, we arrange to meet at a local restaurant.

Day Five

As I pull up to the parking valet, the Rogue is walking toward the restaurant door. I recognize him immediately and am pleased. So pleased, in fact, that I saunter up to him and put my arms around his neck and say, "Nice to meet you." Oh baby, I feel that spark of chemistry…from both of us! *This* will be a fun evening.

The Rogue and I sit down at the bar and he orders a selection of food and wine. Did I eat and drink? I don't recall. All I know is when I put my hand on his knee, he put his over it as if to keep it there. And when I came back from the ladies room and bent over to give him a light kiss, it was difficult for us to pull apart. Unfortunately, he was leaving for Europe the next day. Anticipation for our next meeting began building.

Day Six

The bicoastal exec is on the other coast but frequently travels to my side of the country. After exchanging four emails, I discover he's traveling to Las Vegas at the same time I happen to be going there. Now, isn't that convenient? He invites me for dinner, and volunteers airfare and a hotel room. What the heck...I'm there. It's Vegas, and stranger things have happened in Vegas. He and I have never even spoken on the phone, and I have just one outdated picture of him. Nevertheless, the next day I'm driving to the airport.

Bicoastal Exec is understanding when my flight is delayed three times, but seems a little impatient. Three hours overdue, my car pulls up to the hotel. An elegant man dressed all in black is standing at the curb. One small picture isn't much to go on, so I have to believe he'll know me as I step out of the car. He does – he even comes over and offers his hand to help me out. He walks me to my room, and, leaving me at the door to freshen up for dinner, says he'll return in an hour. In the room is a chilled bottle of champagne and a lovely note welcoming me to Las Vegas.

Bicoastal Exec is hard to read, but fascinating - possibly *because* he's hard to read. We share some champagne and conversation in my room before leaving for dinner. In the restaurant he hands me the wine list and tells me to order whatever I like. Dinner is superb. He turns to me and says with a boyish smile, "I can't stand it. Shall we kiss and get it out of the way?" I grab his lapels and pull him toward me. *Oh. Oh!* That was better than the wine. I have to take a deep breath and stop talking for a minute.

At the end of the night he asks me to stay an additional day, and tells me to go shopping for an outfit while he's working.

Day Seven

I have been so busy since returning from Vegas that I haven't been able to write. When I got home there were many emails to read. MM wanted to fly down and meet for dinner. He sent along a link to a pair of Christian Louboutin shoes that he liked and thought I would as well. He explained that he likes to bring gifts to the first meeting to show he's serious.

I exchanged a few emails with a very nice man living close to my home town. We set up a date to meet but before we could, he met someone that seemed to be a good fit for him.

And then there is GW. We have had a fun ongoing email conversation on SeekingArrangement.com which has turned into something very exciting. GW lives on both coasts and travels to Europe often. He is intelligent, quick-witted and very handsome. He's a very busy man and wanted to meet soon, but was leaving for London in a couple of days. He asked me to meet him in New York and fly on to London with him, which I agreed to do. How exciting! I've never been to London, and was looking forward to meeting him.

As so often happens, plans changed. GW had to stay in New York for business, so we moved our date to Atlanta, where we both happened to be traveling at the same time. We continued our email conversations. After putting together the details of our meeting, he asked if I would perform certain sexual favors – he wanted me to entertain him with four of his business associates. Although I'm comfortable with the expectations of an SD/SB relationship, I have certain boundaries.

This ended our fledgling arrangement. I was very disappointed in GW. I'd thought everything had been going so well. He seemed to be the perfect match for my Sugar Daddy vision. Handsome, in his fifties, intelligent, successful, and classy, with a great sense of humor and – or so I thought from his emails – he understood how to treat his Sugar Baby. It's odd how I never even suspected what his intentions were. And now I feel like he just wanted to meet so he could entertain his associates.

That's okay, I have some other wonderful men to choose from. I'll be seeing the Rogue soon, as he's on his way from Zurich to California. I cannot wait to see his devilish smile. I'm pulling out the little black dress and stilettos, running an extra mile on the jog and getting my nails done. This time he did charter that plane and is coming here. I'm cooking dinner for him. Risotto, red wine, chocolate dessert…maybe on me. Wish me luck!

APPENDIX III

Sugar-Themed Movies

AMERCAN GIGOLO (1980)

Julian makes a lucrative living as an escort to older women in the Los Angeles area. He begins a relationship with Michelle, a local politician's wife, without expecting payment. When one of his clients is murdered, Detective Sunday pumps him for information about his various clients, and he tries to "protect his sources." Eventually Julian suspects he's being framed; meanwhile, Michelle falls in love with him. Probably the first film to openly portray a professional male escort/Sugar Baby. Stars Richard Gere, Lauren Hutton, Nina Van Pallandt. Director: Paul Schrader

DAISIES (1967)

Perpetually dressed in costumes and dark black eyeliner, Marie and Marie decide to "go bad." They stage various dinner dates with stale old men, eat and drink merrily while telling lies, and, in a fast-motion bit of slapstick, hop trains and lose the men. Always looking for new adventures, the girls get drunk at a nightclub and get kicked out in grand style. They sit around their apartment, apathetic to the men professing their love. Pursuing adventure about town, the two Maries take a dumbwaiter up to a banquet hall and proceed to delightfully demolish it. A key film in the Czech New Wave movement, *Daisies* was banned and the director was forbidden to work until 1975. Director: Vera Chytilová.

DIRTY ROTTEN SCOUNDRELS (1988)

Freddy Benson, a con artist, lives off women by awakening their compassion with shocking stories about his phony medical condition. In *Beaumont sur Mer* on the French Mediterranean, he meets Lawrence Jamieson, an older gentleman who works the rich ladies with similar schemes, but is in a much bigger, more sophisticated league. Freddy blackmails Lawrence into teaching him high-society behavior so he can move into that league. After his "education", Freddy decides to stay in town, but since there's no way two con men can work a place so small at the same time, they make a bet to settle the matter - the first one to con $50,000 from a beautiful young female target wins, while the other has to leave town. Wealthy Sugar Mamas, ruthless Sugar Baby wanna-be's. Stars Steve Martin, Michael Caine, Glenne Headly. Director: Frank Oz.

GENTLEMEN PREFER BLONDES (1953)

Lorelei and Dorothy are just "two little girls from Little Rock," who are lounge singers working their way on a transatlantic cruise to Paris. Lorelei is engaged to marry a wealthy man, and Dorothy is supposed to be keeping her away from other men, but she's too dazzled by the half-naked Olympic team on board to see or care what Lorelei does. The two girls get into all kinds of adventures with the wealthy men on the ship. Includes Marilyn Monroe in the knockout musical number "Diamonds are a Girl's Best Friend." Based on the Broadway musical based on the novel. Starring Marilyn Monroe and Jane Russell. Director: Howard Hawks.

HENRY AND JUNE (1990)

Based on a true story. In 1931 Paris, writer Anais Nin meets Henry

Miller while he's writing his first major work, *Tropic of Cancer*, a pseudo-biography of his wife June. Anais is intrigued, and becomes sexually involved, first with Henry and later with June. At the same time, she begins expanding her sexual horizons with her husband Hugo, who helps finance Miller's book. June shuttles between Paris and New York trying to find acting jobs while Anais and Henry argue about writing styles against the backdrop of a Bohemian lifestyle in Paris. Hot, erotic, complex. Possible interpretation as subtle Sugar Daddy/Mama overtones, on a mentor level without the financial component. Based on Nin's book of the same name as well as her journals. Stars Uma Thurman, Maria de Medeiros, Fred Ward, Kevin Spacey. Director: Phillip Kaufman.

HOW TO MARRY A MILLIONAIRE (1953)

Three New York models - Shatze, Pola and Loco – move into a New York penthouse apartment with a Sugar Baby plan: tired of cheap men and a lack of money, they intend to use all their talents to find and marry three millionaires. The trouble is that's it's not so easy to tell the real rich men from the fakes - and even when they can, they wonder if the money's really worth it. Stars Marilyn Monroe, Betty Grable, Lauren Bacall, Rory Calhoun, William Powell. Director: Jean Negulesco.

KLUTE (1971)

After a businessman disappears, the FBI draw a blank except for some letters he wrote to a call-girl. His small-town friend John Klute travels to the city to seek her out. At first their relationship is wary, and she sees him as just another guy to manipulate. But someone may already be stalking her, and as Klute's activities add to the danger, a bond starts to grow between them. Director: Alan Pakula.

MISTRESS (1992)

A comedy about a screenwriter whose old movie script is read by an enthusiastic producer. The search for financial backing begins, but every willing source of money wants his own mistress put into the film. Gradually, the screenwriter is forced to change the script to accommodate the backers until there's no semblance of his original ideas left. Stars Madonna, Robert Wuhl, Martin Landau, Eli Wallach, Danny Aiello, Jean Smart, Robert de Niro. Director: Barry Primus.

MY ONE AND ONLY (2009)

Fresh from his role as the millionaire Mr. Big in *Sex and the City*, Chris Noth will be playing yet another millionaire in *My One and Only*. As a wealthy retired doctor, Noth is targeted by Renee Zellweger as a potential Sugar Daddy to help fund her lifestyle and her children's upbringing. The script is allegedly based on a story actor George Hamilton once told Merv Griffin. Director: Richard Loncraine.

THE OTHER BOLEYN GIRL (2008)

A sensual tale of intrigue, romance and betrayal set against the backdrop of a defining moment in European history, based on real people (events seem to be primarily fictional). Two beautiful sisters, Anne and Mary Boleyn, are driven by their family's blind ambition to compete for the love of the handsome and passionate King Henry VIII. Each of the girl's relationships with the Tudor king has varying Sugar Daddy/Sugar Baby overtones. The relationships are non-consensual: the girls are exploited, humiliated and abused for other people's purposes. Stars Natalie Portman as Anne Boleyn, Scarlett Johannsson as Mary, and Eric Bana as King Henry VIII. Director: Justin Chadwick.

PRETTY WOMAN (1990)

Edward Lewis is a rich, ruthless businessman who specializes in hostile corporate takeovers. In Los Angeles on business one night, he hires a prostitute. They take a liking to each other and he offers her money to stay with him for an entire week so she can accompany him to society parties and polo matches. As they take in the "rich and famous" scene, romance, comedy and complications ensue. Very much the quintessential Hollywood fairy tale. The nice thing about PW is that it doesn't take a disapproving attitude towards the Sugar arrangements on screen, and is even fairly enlightened about prostitution. Stars Julia Roberts, Richard Gere. Director : Garry Marshall.

PRICELESS (2008) French

This French comedy features AMELIE star Audrey Tautou and Gad Elmaleh as Jean, a hardworking employee at an elite resort hotel in southern France. Jean is known for his excellent work ethic, but that changes after a chance encounter with sexy hotel guest Irene (Tautou). Bored with her wealthy and much older boyfriend/benefactor, Irene is looking for excitement. She finds it with Jean, whom she believes to be another guest at the hotel. When she discovers that he's merely an employee, she is furious, and wants nothing more to do with him. She lets him know that she's only interested in men with money—lots and lots of money. Jean is broke and brokenhearted, until he crosses paths with another hotel guest, an older woman of considerable means, and soon finds himself living the high life with his own benefactor. But Jean is far more interested in romance than in riches, and the glitzy fun and games quickly come to a head. French. Stars Audrey Tautou, Gad Elmaleh, Marie-Christine. Director: Andre Joseph.

SECRETARY (2002)

Lee Holloway is a smart, quirky woman in her twenties who returns to her hometown in Florida after a brief stay in a mental hospital. In search of relief from herself and her oppressive childhood environment, she starts to date a nerdy friend from high school and takes a job as a secretary in a local law firm, soon developing an obsessive crush on her older boss, Mr. Grey. Through their sexual S/M relationship, Lee follows her deepest longings to the heights of masochism and finally to a place of self-affirmation. Director: Steven Shainberg.

SHOP GIRL (2005)

Mirabelle is a young aspiring artist who sells gloves and accessories at a department store. Her musician boyfriend goes on tour about the same time as the wealthy sixty-something Ray Porter finds her at the glove counter, and her life takes a magical turn. But Ray thinks he's made it clear it's just an affair, while she hears more. Slight Sugar Daddy/Sugar Baby relationship. Stars Steve Martin, Claire Danes, Jason Schwartzman. Director: Anand Tucker. Based on the book of the same name by Steve Martin.

SOME LIKE IT HOT (1959)

Two struggling musicians witness the St. Valentine's Day Massacre and flee Chicago so they won't be killed by the mob. The only job that will pay their way out of the city is an all-girl band, so they go in drag. Joe, the saxophone player, poses as Josephine, and Jerry, the bass violin player, becomes Daphne. Joe, aka Josephine, falls in love with Sugar Kane, a ukelele player and singer who's always getting into trouble with booze and men. After a train ride that sets a record for number of people in an upper berth, they reach Miami, where Joe decides to pose as an oil billionaire to capture Sugar's heart. He invites her onto "his" yacht, owned by Osgood Fielding, while "Daphne" distracts Osgood on shore. The pace gets even giddier when the Chicago mob arrives in Miami for a convention. This is a hilarious movie, far ahead of its time in terms of representations of gender fluidity and sexual orientation. Marilyn has never been more delicious. Starring Marilyn Monroe, Tony Curtis, Jack Lemmon. Director: Billy Wilder.

THE LOVER (1992)

Set against the backdrop of French colonial Vietnam, The Lover reveals the intimacies and intricacies of a clandestine romance between a young girl (Jane March) from a financially strapped French family and an older, wealthy Chinese man (Tony Leung Ka-Fai). The story is narrated by Jeanne Moreau, portraying a writer looking back on her youth. Compelled by the circumstances of her upbringing, this girl, the daughter of a bankrupt, manic-depressive widow, is newly awakened to the impending and all-too-real task of making her way alone in the world. Thus, she becomes his lover, until an arranged marriage forces him into a choice between tradition, family, and honor on the one hand, and a love that he claims to be "too weak" to pursue on the other. For her lover, there is no question of the depth and sincerity of his love, but it isn't until much later that the girl acknowledges to herself her true feelings. Starring Jane March and Tony Leung Ka Fai. Director: Jean-Jacques Annaud

Appendix IV:

Prostitution versus Arrangements

Every time I'm interviewed by the media, I invariably get asked the same question: What makes Sugar Daddy/Baby relationships different from prostitution? To my mind, it's self-evident that mutually beneficial relationships are a world apart from the oldest profession in the world – but I've had to think long and hard about the issue in order to articulate the differences.

To most people, any coupling of sex-and-money apparently equals prostitution. It's not only Sugar arrangements that bear this stigma: sex therapists, sex surrogates, and platonic escorts, to name just a few professions, get accused of prostitution, not as a neutral, descriptive word, but as a nasty epithet. In the case of mutually beneficial arrangements, several significant differences prove the epithet false, to wit:

- Most prostitutes engage in sex for money with almost anyone who hires them. If she doesn't like his looks, his personality, or his smell, she's not likely to turn him down, and if she works for an agency, she can't.

  But in the sugar-daddy/sugar-baby relationship, there's no guarantee of sex. As with any other relationship freely entered into, each partner decides whether to engage in sexual activity. Most Sugar Babies say there has to be chemistry on some level between her and a man in order for the relationship to become sexual.

- Prostitutes who work the streets find their clients there. Most of the time, they've never seen the man before. Call girls who work for agencies get sent to do a job for men they've never met. It's work.

In a sugar-daddy/sugar-baby relationship, the woman usually has a great deal of contact with the man prior to meeting, and determines, based on phone conversations and photo exchange, if she wants to see him in person. These are online dating interactions, with the difference that the men are wealthy, and the women are more attractive than on most dating websites. Built into the relationship is the expectation that the man will pamper the woman; most of these men do this naturally, no matter how or where they've met their dates.

- Prostitutes charge a set amount of money prior to sex, with various fees added according to the sexual activities the man asks for. She is expected to accommodate any fairly reasonable requests.

Any money or gifts a Sugar Daddy gives a Sugar Baby are freely presented at any time, not as payment for sex. Ideally, financial agreements are finalized at the outset of the relationship, and it's understood that the money is not a sex fee, but given out of generosity and a desire to help the woman.

About The Author

Brandon Wade is founder and CEO of the websites SeekingArrangement.com and SeekingMillionaire.com. As an entrepreneur, he's started numerous internet and mobile companies, as well as retail and tour businesses. Prior to these endeavors, he served as a management consultant with Booz Allen, and held executive roles at several Fortune 500 companies, including General Electric and Microsoft.

Originally from Singapore, Wade moved to the United States to study at the Massachusetts Institute of Technology, from which he graduated with a BS and an MBA degree. Since then, he has lived in Boston, New York, Seattle, New Orleans and San Francisco (all Sugar Daddy dating capitols, by the way). He has been married twice, and resides in Las Vegas with his wife - Sugar Baby Numero Uno - Yulyia, and their beloved Chihuahua.

Acknowledgements

I would like to thank everyone who helped to make the creation of this book a reality. In particular, I'd like to thank my assistant, Stephan Smith, who was instrumental in helping me coordinate this book and see it through from start to finish. Alicia Dunams, my project manager, helped turn this book from idea to reality. Writer Marcy Sheiner's ideas, feedback and contribution helped to shape this book. Darren Shuster from Pop Culture PR who helped me with many of the concepts in this book. My family, including my wife, sister, mother and father, encouraged me along the way. Most of all, members of SeekingArrangement.com gave me the inspiration and materials for this book.

Thank you one and all.

Now that you have read the book,
come experience the lifestyle for yourself!

I'm offering readers an exclusive free trial
membership to SeekingArrangement.com.

To redeem this offer, please visit the following
website and follow the registration instructions:

http://www.seekingarrangement.com/book/offer.php

SeekingArrangement.com

Made in the USA
Middletown, DE
08 March 2022

62337063R00158